# AUCAS DOWNRIVER

ETHEL EMILY WALLIS

# ✲ AUCAS

HARPER & ROW, PUBLISHERS

# DOWNRIVER

## DAYUMA'S STORY TODAY

NEW YORK, EVANSTON, SAN FRANCISCO, LONDON

FIRST EDITION

STANDARD BOOK NUMBER: 06–069212–x

LIBRARY OF CONGRESS CATALOG CARD NUMBER: 72–9873

*To Woody and Beryl Adcock*
*"who have ministered to the Saints"*

 CONTENTS

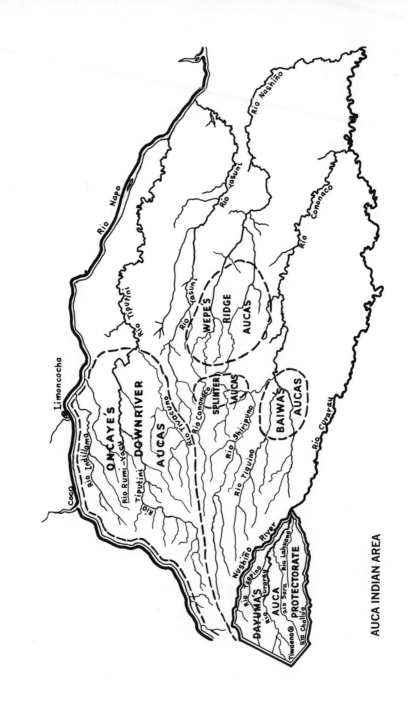

AUCA INDIAN AREA

 PREFACE

"What happened to the Indians who killed those five missionaries?" This question is frequently asked by concerned Christians around the world who remember the bloody scenes of "Palm Beach" in 1956. In *The Dayuma Story* a beginning of miracles in the murderous Auca tribe of Ecuador was recounted, but greater things have happened since I left South America in 1960 after having completed the post-Palm Beach story. The present narrative of current Auca history will, I trust, even more positively affirm the worth of a costly sacrifice made by five dedicated men and their families.

Because of the circumstances that accorded me the privilege of writing the "inside" Auca story, this account will focus upon Wycliffe translator Rachel Saint, sister of pilot Nate Saint, one of the five slain by Auca spears.

Inextricably intertwined, however, is the role played by other pilots, those of Wycliffe's Jungle Aviation and Radio Service, who in the tradition of Nate Saint, of the Missionary Aviation Fellowship, are completely committed to a God-assigned task in a jungle where danger is a daily companion. Without the risks taken by these and other consecrated technicians, the acts presented in this book would not have happened.

Jungle pilots do more than fly planes over desolate areas; they also keep good records. Recently, to confirm the facts regarding a crucial flight in February, 1964, I called pilot Merrill Piper long distance and asked for data. Within minutes he flipped to a page in his Log Book, lying within reach, and gave me precise and exciting details. During that historic flight the first down-river clearing was discovered from the air by Aucas in the plane with Piper. Upon that event hinged the subsequent developments recounted in the following pages. Thank God for pilots who also keep good records!

To another pilot and his wife, I am deeply indebted. Veteran airlines pilot Roy Long and his wife, Martha, graciously hosted Rachel and me in their Florida home and thus enabled us to complete the manuscript in ideal surroundings. To other Wycliffe friends who generously donated their time for typing, I am grateful. Dorothy Krauter and Ruby Rogers invested hours in typing taped information, which provided background for much of the story. Gwen Frost budgeted her time to type the final manuscript while caring for an active family.

To Eleanor Jordan, Harper & Row editor and faithful friend, I am once again grateful. Her creative assistance in the production of *The Dayuma Story* issued in a host of appreciative readers. I am confident that they and others will reap the benefits of her sure touch in *Aucas Downriver*.

ETHEL EMILY WALLIS

# AUCAS DOWNRIVER

# 1 ❧ BLOODSHED ON FATHER RIVER

Tidonca's poison dart hit its target, high in the towering jungle trees that all but concealed his small clearing. Expert hunter that he was, he had tilted his blowgun at a sharp angle, aimed at the spot where his keen eyes had spied the *gata* monkey half-hidden in the top branches. With a mighty puff, measured precisely for distance and target, he had hit the monkey squarely. The animal slumped and dropped limply to a lower branch, still high above the cramped clearing below, choked all around by dark, thick forest.

"Oncaye!" Tidonca called to his little half-sister. "Get the monkey and bring it down!"

Old Grandmother Boika was already blowing up the ground fire to singe the woolly monkey and cook it in the big clay pot.

The slim, supple body of the naked young Auca girl was soon slithering up the giant tree. Having loosely bound her ankles together with a length of jungle vine as a climbing ring, she was shortly out of sight and reaching for the monkey. As she was about to grab it, she heard a buzzing noise, which she thought was a bumblebee near her head. But no, it was too loud, and it zoomed louder and nearer. What was it? It wasn't a jungle noise. Now it was directly overhead. She was terrified. Oh! It was that foreigners' Thing that had crossed the sky above the clearing several times lately! It came even closer and louder. There were *people* in it! Then with a mighty roar it was gone, out of sight.

*Oh, why didn't I look well to see if those were our people in that Thing? Why didn't I look well?*

As Oncaye chided herself, the Thing came again, flying close

1

and low. Trembling with fear, she stretched herself to the tip of the limb for a good look.

*Our people with big holes in their earlobes*—Aucas!

Oncaye saw the two Auca faces clearly. She had never been beyond Father River where the foreigners lived, but she knew that big earholes were the mark of her people. A few Aucas had fled the spearings of her tribe and gone to the outside where the cannibals—Eaters-of-People—lived. *Perhaps they had not all been eaten alive. Were some of them in that Thing that whizzed by?*

Oncaye was so excited she almost forgot the monkey draped over the limb above her. She turned back, grabbed the dark woolly animal, and slid down the tree trunk. She ran into the clearing, calling breathlessly, "Our people were in that foreigners' Thing! I *saw* them from the top of the tree . . . there were *holes* in their ears!"

"Stop talking wild, Oncaye!" her mother, Titada, scolded from under the big thatched roof. "That was a *devil* flying in the sky! What makes you say that there were real people in it?"

"But they *were* real people . . . they were Aucas!" Oncaye insisted. "I saw them plainly with my own eyes, and I saw the big holes in their ears!"

"Looking at the Thing, you saw the souls of the foreigners we speared on the banks of Father River," Tidonca said. "In front of the Thing there are arms that go around like this . . ." and he demonstrated, flailing his muscular arms like a human windmill. "Their arms go like this, and their souls are in that Thing. That's what you saw."

Oncaye was laughed at and taunted for her ignorance. But the young girl could not be dissuaded. She could not forget the clear view of Auca faces in the Thing that almost touched the top of the tree where the *gata* monkey had fallen.

That night in her hammock, as the night monkeys chattered and the soft wind teased the lazy fire into a final burst of flame, Oncaye thought again of the faces she had seen in the sky.

Her people, who were trying desperately to hide from enemy groups of their own tribe and from outsiders now crossing their boundaries, had huddled downriver in this tiny clearing in Ecuador's eastern jungle, eating monkey meat and fishing in a nearby stream. Their manioc fields were skimpy and half-hidden, hopefully not to be spotted by foreigners' Things that flew over them. Sometimes when they had gone downstream to fish, outsiders had stolen the manioc right out of their fields.

One day away was Father River, or Big River—the Napo to outsiders—running eastward toward the Amazon. The Napo and Curaray Rivers had traditionally marked the borders where a few hundred savage Indians were defending their rain-forest homeland at spearpoint.

From 1542, when Orellana had gone down the Napo to the mighty Amazon, until now, February, 1964, the battle with outsiders had continued. Sharp, hard spears made from the ironlike wood of the chonta palm had formed an effective weapon against them.

Recently, the battle had become hotter as outsiders became bolder in their attempts to enter the Aucas' land. Strange Things were increasing in the sky overhead. The flying devils would even dip down to see what Aucas were doing. But this time Oncaye knew they were *Aucas* in the sky!

Hatred for all outsiders was a long-standing law of the tribe. Oncaye's stepfather, Niwa, often reviewed for her sake the well-known tales of the ancestors about the *cowode*, the foreigners, Eaters-of-People. The ancestors had long since established that the Eaters-of-People had a magic Thing called a *caento*. It made a loud noise, and then the *cowode* just reached out and grabbed their victims, who of course were Aucas. The Eaters-of-People lopped off Auca flesh with their big foreign knives, roasted it and ate it. They painted the blood on the magic *caento*, saying, "This is your share." Thus the helpless Aucas died, hacked to pieces little by little. Niwa said:

"The Aucas had gone to get palm fiber when they heard the

Thing screaming, 'Eat, eat, eat!' Suddenly, Aucas were captured and kept under guard. From time to time the Eaters-of-People would come and carry off some of the captive Aucas. 'What's going on?' cried the few remaining Aucas. 'They're eating all of us! Soon there won't be one of us left!'

"And so the Aucas fled back to their homeland, across Father River, where they lay in wait for the Killers-of-People who would follow.

"The Aucas watched until they came over a hill. When the last one was in sight, the Aucas yelled *'Badogaa*—after 'em—' and they showered them with a volley of spears. The *cowode* ran screaming, scattering in all directions. The Aucas pursued them down to the water. They killed lots and lots of them, those worthless *cowode!* But some of the *cowode* took a flying leap and landed in the treetops. You could see them up there with their clothes on, the ancestors said. So the Aucas threw their spears up and killed them too.

"A few of the *cowode* escaped. 'Follow them, let's kill them all,' the Aucas said, 'and destroy the magic *caento,* the Thing that screams, and makes them grab us, eat and kill us.'

"The Aucas returned to the foreigners' houses and bashed the Thing to pieces, using the foreigners' own axes.

" 'Now there are just a few of us,' the Aucas said. 'Fleeing, we must go far upriver. There's nothing else to do! Perhaps there we can live well.' So they did, but they often said, 'We think of our relatives with great sorrow. We are so few—the foreigners ate many of us.' "

At night in their hammocks the Aucas sang the songs of the ancestors, the nasal, monotonous chants which repeated familiar refrains about foreigners infringing upon the rights of the Aucas:

> Like stars coming out, the foreigners came,
> One here, one there, and another one yonder
> Like rain clouds, we will blot them out!

Foreigners were not the only ones killed. From a small child Oncaye had heard about many spearings among her people. She often wondered about her own father who had been speared when she was a baby. She herself had almost been thrown alive in the grave with him. Many times she had heard how Grandmother Boika snatched her from that hideous death. She shuddered to think that she herself might have been *buried alive with her father.*

Since that day she had slept with her grandmother in the hammock. The firm, kind hands of Boika, roughened by planting manioc and carrying firewood, had often consoled the Auca child, frightened at night by shouting and spearing. Even now she could remember being cradled by day in a bark-cloth sling at her grandmother's breast or standing as Boika lovingly combed the tangles from her long shiny black hair. When it grew down over Oncaye's eyes, she carefully chopped short bangs with a sharp clamshell pressed against hard chonta wood as a cutting board. It was Boika who had pierced her grandchild's ears with a big sharp thorn and gradually expanded the holes in her earlobes by wedging into the perforation a rolled jungle leaf. How the juice of those rough leaves pained and stung the raw flesh! But they stretched open the holes, making room for successively larger white balsa earplugs, the mark of Auca womanhood.

Oncaye now slept in her own hammock, but on dark nights when her brothers were angry and talking wild, she wished she could slip into Boika's hammock to feel again the comfort of warm bare flesh against her own small trembling body. But she was becoming a woman and must be brave. She would have to learn to live, and perhaps to flee, all by herself.

The men talked of spearing the foreigners who had found the trail right to their houses. One day when the men had returned from hunting, they saw the foreigners' footprints nearby. Oncaye's half-brother, Dabu, was furious.

"Having killed them, we will return!" Each Auca killer

heeded this signal to make spears, notched with his own special barbs. They marched through the forest, quickly felled the balsa trees and chopped the logs for a raft. These were lashed together with vines, and then poles of wild cane were cut for pushing the raft through the small river blocked by jungle growth. Soon the Aucas poled their way to Father River. Stationing themselves in a thick grove of trees on the riverbank, they watched until two Quichua Indians with a small girl appeared on the opposite bank and prepared to enter a canoe. Quickly splashing through the water, the Aucas then plunged their spears into the Quichuas, who had no time to retaliate. They grabbed the small child, swam back to their side of the river, and disappeared among the big trees.

When they returned to the isolated clearing, Oncaye listened to the details of the ambush. She pitied the frightened captive and tried to comfort her. Since the small foreigner spoke no Auca, Oncaye had to use gestures. The child began to relax and ate the food offered to her.

Dabu and the other killers, still enraged, talked far into the night around the fire.

Just as life was resuming a normal routine of blowgunning monkeys and harvesting manioc, word came of more foreigners crossing their borders farther downriver. The brothers again made spears hastily and plotted their attack. But now there was trouble within the family group. Oncaye's Aunt Nimu had been frustrated in marriage plans and was angry with her family. She decided to escape to the outside world of the cannibals and take her chances there. When her brothers were ready to leave, they consented to take Nimu with them. They insisted on having the captured girl along. Perhaps her presence would improve Nimu's chances with the outsiders.

As the spearing party approached the Big River, the brothers sent the small child ahead. Nimu followed. They crossed the river on foot near the place where the two Quichuas had been killed, the Auca men watching from a safe distance on their side of the river.

As soon as Nimu and the child reached the foreigners' side, a loud shot rang out, and the child dropped to the ground. Another shot, and Nimu slumped.

The Aucas could hardly believe their own eyes. The foreigners had killed one of their own! And Nimu had not even been given a chance! Shocked and angry, the brothers waited until they were sure there would be no more shooting. Finally, they crossed the river, swiftly recovered Nimu's body, and buried it in a hollow log near the riverbank. They did not touch the child's body.

The men returned home, where they continued to scream and brandish spears.

"Why did those hateful foreigners kill Nimu?" Dabu yelled.

Old Boika in her hammock trembled at his voice and hugged a tiny great-grandchild close to her thin body. She feared the consequences of Dabu's anger, now out of control.

"Why should Nimu be killed, and a worthless old woman still live?" he shrieked. He lunged toward Boika with his spear.

"Don't spear—don't spear me!" screamed the terrified woman.

Tidonca tore the baby from her arms and tossed it to the child's father. Then he plunged the spear through Boika's body, impaling her flesh through the hammock to the ground.

Oncaye fled. She crouched behind a big tree, listening to her grandmother's dying groans. Her heart thumped and her slight body shook with stifled sobs.

"Grandmother—my own Grandmother Boika—why did my brother spear her?" She wanted to run, run far away into the dark forest, but it was night, and she didn't know the trail, and there were snakes and jaguars . . .

It was long after midnight when Oncaye crept back to the bloody scene of Boika's death. Her mother, Titada, was still weeping and wailing loudly. All night the clearing echoed with outbursts of grief and loud Auca chants of fury.

Oncaye sobbed softly to herself. *Why do my people live so badly? Why do they live, only killing and spearing?*

Life was never the same after Boika's death. Oncaye helped dig the manioc roots and cook the monkeys which her brothers dropped with their blowguns, but she was wary. There had been rumors of threats on Niwa's life. And if Niwa were speared, she would have no protection from enemies within Niwa's large family, who would surely capture her and carry her away.

Oncaye began to plot her own course of action. She would flee to the outside when she had a chance. Even the risk of the outsiders' weapons would be better than being speared in your hammock!

One day she heard her brothers talking of another spearing trip on the river. When she asked to go with them, they agreed. She followed them on the trail until they came to the area where they would again make a balsa raft for the journey. Soon they were on their way.

As the water splashed rhythmically against the raft, Oncaye thought of what lay ahead. There were cannibals, killers, enemies, on the outside.

*Will they kill me, as they did Aunt Nimu? Will they lop off my flesh in big chunks and eat me alive?*

She could turn back, return to the fight in the forest, to the spearings and hatred in her own family groups scattered upriver and downriver in the jungle that hid them from each other. Her small body stiffened with determination.

*I'll go to the outside, never to return. I'll go once for all, and if I die, I'll die!*

They reached the Big River. Swimming across it, her brothers led the way to the spot where they had buried Nimu.

To their horror they found that her corpse had been pulled out of the hollow log, mutilated, and scattered on the ground where it continued to rot. The foreigners had inflicted the worst possible insult: leaving a body to rot above the ground. The Auca men were more furious than ever.

At that moment some foreign men appeared at the bend of the river. The brothers, after thrusting Oncaye ahead of them toward the men, turned and ran. Then they watched from a hiding place in the forest.

*No one would attack a winsome young girl!*

There were angry shouts. Oncaye darted toward the forest like a scared deer. She ducked behind a fallen tree. A shot rang out. Oncaye felt a sharp pain in her leg. She fell to the ground, writhing in agony.

Her brothers burst forth to her rescue, only to be met by more fire. Wounded but able to run, they fled, leaving Oncaye alone, the strength fast draining from her limp body . . .

# 2 ❀ TO SPEAR NO MORE

Tiwaeno, lying at the bend of Chonta Palm River for which it was named, was the first settled Auca community in Ecuador. Located upriver at the headwaters of Amazon tributaries not far from the foot of the Andes, Tiwaeno was now clearly visible from the air. The Aucas here made no attempt to hide from foreigners who flew over in airplanes. The small river on which they lived fed into the Curaray, which in turn flowed into the larger Napo. Together downstream these rivers joined the Amazon, that giant of all rivers which three thousand miles away to the east emptied into the Atlantic.

Against a backdrop of lush, matted jungle was a grassy airstrip the size of a football field, which formed the center of the progressive Indian settlement. Large thatched houses stood clumped together at one end of the elliptical bald spot on the jungle floor. The airstrip, adequate for skilled jungle pilots only, had opened an aerial gateway to the foreigners' world for the first time in a long bloody history.

For centuries Aucas had speared the outsiders—Quichua Indians, remnants of the old Inca empire; Spanish conquerors; and more recently, prospectors from afar seeking rubber, oil, and gold. But Tiwaeno was a *new* Auca village.

❀ Heavy night mist still clung to the dense forest surrounding the settlement. Suddenly, the eerie silence was broken by the flap-flap-flap of the *cowatai* bird. It was the muffled jungle alarm preceding the dawn. The strong

Ecuadorian sun would soon be forcing its rays through the blanket of mist.

By dawn the jungle was alive with a wild reveille as every living thing screeched and screamed, scolding the Tiwaeno Aucas still lying in their hammocks around their smoldering ground fires. One by one the Indians began to stir. A brawny Auca man barely visible in the dawning light sat up slowly in his hammock, fanned the embers of his fire into flame, and warmed his big hands by the bright blaze that sprang up. Other Aucas yawned noisily and poked at their fires, which flared up here and there under the cluster of thatched roofs.

It was sunup on a bright Sunday morning in November, 1963 —time to gather at the edge of the clearing in the newly thatched shelter, God's-speaking-house. There the Aucas would hear words in their own language from God's Carving—the written Scriptures—a new code for these Indians whose lives for centuries had been dominated by witchcraft and demons.

Not too long ago these Aucas had laid aside their sharp chonta wood spears fashioned for human slaughter. Their last big raid had occurred in 1956 on a sandy beach of the Curaray River. There a band of killers speared five young Americans who had landed in a small plane within their borders. True, the outsiders had appeared friendly enough at first. But who could tell what lay behind the benign smiles and gentle actions? After all, foreigners were cannibals; the Auca ancestors had warned them thoroughly. The intruders were speared. Later, other foreigners came and buried them.

The Aucas returned to a new hideout and eventually life became routine again.

Two years after the massacre a young Auca girl, Dayuma, who long before had fled to the outside, reappeared on the Auca clearing. Her family were stunned. They had been sure that she was eaten by the foreign cannibals!

Dayuma, as a young adolescent, had decided to flee after her

father was killed. With a cousin about her own age she escaped
to the edge of the Auca forest. Befriended by foreigners, the
two naked Indian girls were taken to a hacienda in the Andean
foothills.

For eight years Dayuma had labored there, harvesting bananas from sun to sun. She adopted the speech and dress of
Quichua Indians, the predominant race of Ecuador's eastern
jungle.

Dayuma's mother had always hoped for her return. She even
called to the Things that flew overhead, "Does my daughter
Dayuma still live?" There had been no answer.

But Dayuma had now come home with two curious aunts
who had ventured to the edge of the jungle and through an
amazing turn of events had found her. "Come home!" they had
urged her. "Your mother still lives!"

Dayuma told her Tiwaeno family unbelievable tales about
outsiders as they gathered to hear her. She regaled them with
stories too strange to be true.

"You're talking wild!" some told her. But they listened, since
she spoke with eyewitness authority.

"Not all foreigners are bad . . . there are some good ones!"
Dayuma told her surprised family. "I have been living with one
of the good ones."

Dayuma was referring to Rachel Saint, a Wycliffe Bible translator. Rachel was the sister of pilot Nate Saint whose small
yellow plane had carried the five men to a beach on the Curaray. When in 1956 Dayuma had been shown the pictures of the
Indians taken by the men on "Palm Beach"—the foreigners'
name for the spot—she knew for the first time in eight years
that her people still lived somewhere near her childhood clearing.

She had also viewed the movies made by the men just before
they were killed, and as she watched, she almost climbed
through the screen, frantic to see more. *Those are my people!
There is my aunt! . . . And my sister!* There was the sandbar by

the river where she had fished and played as a child—but now the beach was *longer*. Long enough for the foreigners' Thing to land on it. Her searching eyes scanned the tall trees in the pictures. The foreigners had built a small house high up in the branches!

Dayuma had studied the faces in the pictures retrieved from Palm Beach after the death of the men. Excited and nostalgic, she began to talk of going home.

"Would your people kill me if I went to them?" Rachel had asked Dayuma.

"Not if you speak our language," she had answered.

Rachel had met Dayuma in 1955 at the jungle hacienda. At that time Nate Saint of the Missionary Aviation Fellowship and four missionary friends were quietly attempting to contact the elusive Aucas. After an apparently successful meeting on the Curaray, the Indians suddenly killed Rachel's brother and his companions.

By the time of their death in January, 1956, Rachel had gradually teased Dayuma back into memory of her native language, using gestures in a monolingual effort to aid the girl's recall. Slowly, Dayuma remembered words, then phrases, then whole sentences of the language of death she had tried to forget.

Besides the news of the outside world, Dayuma told the Aucas stranger tales from God's Carving, which she declared was the true word from heaven. Jesus, God's good Son, had come down to earth long ago. Coming, He was killed, speared by His own people.

"Just as you killed the foreigners on the beach, that's the way they killed Him," Dayuma had told her people. "Not understanding, you killed them. They were good foreigners, they came to tell you about God."

At first her people only laughed at her words. There was one, however, who did not ridicule.

Dawa was a newcomer in Tiwaeno, a young Auca woman

who had not been there when Dayuma fled to the outside. She came later, captured by the Tiwaeno group when they went on a spearing raid downriver. Dawa had seen some of her own family speared before her eyes.

She listened carefully and eagerly to Dayuma's message. Long after the others had gone to their hammocks, Dawa plied her with questions. And she didn't laugh at the "wild" stories about Jesus, that wonderful Son of God, who even walked on the water!

Night after night around the fire Dayuma recounted with gestures and animated Auca intonation all that Rachel had taught her from God's Carving. *God created everything . . . He created us, He even created the foreigners . . . He is thatching a house for us in heaven. Believing, we can enter. Believing, we must follow God's trail.* Stories of Abraham and Joseph and David were embellished with loud and appropriate sound effects improvised by Dayuma, whose teaching captivated her audience. The killers listened, and wondered at this fresh, foreign news.

*Abraham sinned—but God forgave him. David sinned greatly—but God forgave him. Jesus' blood has dripped for us —God forgives us . . .*

Gikita, the oldest man in Tiwaeno, began to listen to Dayuma's teaching. He knew well the teachings of the ancestors about the jaguar and the devil and magic termites, but the words from God's Carving were utterly new. His keen black eyes studied Dayuma's face as she talked, and he weighed every word. His big, perforated earlobes that held balsa earplugs framed his lined, wrinkled face as he sat motionless by the fire.

A month after Dayuma's return, Rachel and Elisabeth Elliot, the widow of one of the five murdered men, together with her small daughter, Valerie, entered the tribe. They were escorted by Dayuma into the Tiwaeno clearing after she had prepared her family to receive them in peace. The Indians, though wary, thatched shelters for the women. For the first time foreigners hung their hammocks with a group of Auca killers who had never allowed outsiders to live in their midst.

Gikita now listened to Rachel, who had come already speaking the language she had learned from Dayuma. Her words about God's Carving were fascinating.

Rachel, Dayuma's close friend, was adopted into the Auca family and called by an Auca name, Nimu, meaning "star."

Gikita would often sit in the shadows and study Nimu's face. It was Gikita, the leader of the killers, who had speared Nimu's brother on the Curaray riverbank. Nate had held his hands high over his head, pleading for mercy, but mercy was not shown.

"Not understanding, I killed Nimu's brother," Gikita said after he decided to accept God's Carving. "But Jesus' blood has washed my heart clean. I used to be hateful but now my heart is healed."

His hands too became clean, for Gikita declared that he no longer intended to spear foreigners or his own people.

*God says, "Don't kill." Loving, we should live well.*

But Kimo, another of the Palm Beach killers, challenged Dayuma's teaching. How could one live in the forest without killing, now that foreigners were intruding? As a boy he had been taught to kill; he had practiced spearing the spongy trunks of banana trees, rolling them down the slopes toward the river as he shouted in mock rage, driving the spear into the soft, easily penetrable stalks. As a young man he had been taken on raids with older men and practiced on live victims, the bodies of those who had been mortally wounded by the older, stronger killers.

Kimo had gone downriver with Gikita to avenge the death of Dayuma's brother and uncle. Shouting and raging, Kimo plunged his spear into Dawa's father. Her mother, wailing in grief and terror, made no effort to flee.

"Let me alone to die!" she had sobbed in her hammock. But Gikita and Kimo showed her no mercy.

"Why did you spear my mother?" Dawa had cried in anguish as she witnessed the brutal murder of her own mother.

Dawa had then been captured as a marriageable young woman and taken to Tiwaeno. Later, Dawa became Kimo's wife.

As a young wife Dawa had watched Kimo spear again. From the opposite bank of the Curaray she looked on as he and Gikita, aided by three others from their group, Nimonga, Minkayi, and Dyuwi, speared the five foreigners. The brutal scene was like the massacre of her own parents, except that the victims were now fair-skinned young men.

Dawa cringed whenever she heard her husband sharpening his spears. Whom would he kill next? She hated spearing and killing and fleeing into the forest to escape reprisals.

God's Carving fell on good ground in Dawa's heart; the message was welcome, for she was weary of bloodshed. She longed for comfort and release from hatred and retaliation, the only law which her people knew. But Kimo resisted the new teaching and he still hated foreigners. The ancestors never said anything like this!

One day Dawa shared with Rachel her concern for Kimo.

"What shall I do?" Dawa asked. "Kimo does not want to believe in Jesus."

Pushed beyond her growing ability in the Auca language, Rachel attempted an answer.

"God's Carving tells us, 'Believing, you shall be saved, and also those in your family,' " she told her. "We will pray and God will help Kimo to believe."

Rachel taught Dawa to talk to God, and to expect His answer.

Eventually, Kimo's hostility lessened, and even the hard lines around his mouth began to relax as he listened to Dayuma.

Young Dyuwi and Nimonga at first resented the presence of foreigners among them. Dyuwi hated all outsiders ever since as a young boy he had been wounded by their gunfire and nearly died. The two younger men feared reprisals and trusted no one from the outside.

Their prejudice began to fade as they observed Gikita and Kimo.

In time Kimo suggested that the group gather at his house to hear God's Carving. Soon Dyuwi joined the others who went to Kimo's whenever Dayuma talked about God.

Dayuma taught her people about the "wood-bees," the foreigners' Things that flew in the sky. Some of the Aucas had seen Nate's little plane at close range on Palm Beach.

Following the massacre they had seen another "wood-bee" flying low over them. The Aucas marveled that after they had killed the five foreigners, good gifts were still being dropped to them from a "wood-bee."

Later, after Rachel's arrival, Dayuma was thrilled to get a close look at the bucket let down by a "vine" from the plane. This was the only contact with the outside. The bucket brought mail and other provisions.

Dayuma eventually persuaded her people to make a landing field. She convinced them that air contact was worth the risk involved in bringing foreign men into the clearing. The Aucas had now begun to believe that not all foreigners were cannibals, but they were slower to believe that outsiders could be trusted.

After the decision to clear the strip, a year of brutally hard labor was required to complete it. Huge jungle trees had to be chopped down with hand axes, their great roots dug out and towed away. With only seven adult men to work on the project, progress was slow. Dayuma encouraged women and children to do their share, so the field was finally cleared.

Pilot Don Smith of Wycliffe's JAARS—Jungle Aviation and Radio Service—had watched the work on the Tiwaeno airfield as he flew over occasionally. He now felt that he could land safely on the 600-foot strip. "But the decision to allow the pilot to land was mine," Rachel remembers. "I thought of what had happened to Nate and his friends; the photos of his mutilated plane were clear in my mind. Dayuma and I felt sure that her regular teaching from God's Carving had changed the hearts of the killers in our midst, but no outside *man* had ever left Auca territory unscathed.

"I'll never forget the expression of wonder on the Aucas' faces as they watched the plane come in for the first landing."

Before the plane left there was a prayer of thanksgiving in English. Dyuwi then prayed in Auca, giving thanks to the God of heaven who had allowed this day to come to pass, the day when Auca men and foreign men could meet together in peace.

Air service spelled progress for the work on several fronts. In May, 1961, Kimo and Minkayi and their wives flew with Rachel and Dayuma to Wycliffe's jungle base at Limoncocha, on the Napo River, for a linguistic workshop under the direction of Dr. Kenneth L. Pike. A milestone was passed when the Auca alphabet was officially approved and Rachel was encouraged by Pike to undertake the translation of the Gospel of Mark.

In August, 1962, the plane served a special purpose. Dayuma, who had been married to a Quichua Indian when she lived at the hacienda, had been left a widow with her small son, Sammy. Now Dayuma was to become the bride of Komi, son of Gikita. Since she had lived on the outside, Dayuma's wedding was to be different. Ordinarily, a prospective Auca bride knows neither that a groom has been selected for her nor that there is to be a ceremony until she is taken to the hammock where she is to be married. Arrangements are made by the two families involved.

Excitement was in the air when the plane landed. Soon Don Smith was informed that he would participate in the wedding.

"But what shall I do?" he asked Rachel, realizing that he lacked the necessary practice for such an occasion.

"Just do whatever the Auca men do, and follow their lead," Rachel told him.

Don galloped around the airstrip with the Auca men in a traditional wedding dance that ended under a thatched roof where Dayuma sat beaming in a hammock. The willing groom was plunked down beside her. The men then chanted the wedding song, Don squatting beside Dayuma's Uncle Gikita. "Now you are married!" they sang. The song ended, Dyuwi and Don asked the Lord's blessing on the marriage.

Rachel recalls: "Later I learned that Don had taken the place of Dayuma's father who had been speared years before, and that he had officially performed the marriage!"

A wedding meal followed at Rachel's house. Dayuma, who had learned outside the tribe to eat at a table, instructed Komi, who was eating at a table for the first time. In a constant undertone she coached him. *Just take one piece of chicken at first, only one piece of bread . . . pour some of that on your rice . . .*

Rachel had even made a wedding cake, which Dayuma and Komi cut together. She wrote of the event:

"When I watched Komi trying to eat canned peach halves with a spoon, I wondered about my choice of a wedding dessert. But a happy time was had by all, especially by Dayuma, who had her heart set on a very special wedding, and by Komi, who had his heart set on Dayuma."

The following year the airstrip served a more somber purpose when the small plane became an ambulance for Dayuma. The birth of baby Nancy "Hummingbird," begun in Auca fashion in a jungle hammock, became complicated. The birth was completed in Shell Mera at the edge of the jungle, where missionaries of radio station HCJB have a hospital. Nancy's thus became the first Auca birth to be officially registered in Ecuador.

In the critical hours when Dayuma's life was in danger, Rachel had silently entreated God to spare her experienced translation helper. Dayuma's teaching talent had produced strong believers, spiritual soldiers in training for the battles that lay ahead.

Rachel was doubly grateful to have Dayuma with her charming black-eyed baby daughter finally back in Tiwaeno.

Other changes had also occurred in Tiwaeno. In 1963 Betty Elliot and little Valerie had returned to the United States, and Catherine Peeke, a Wycliffe partner who had worked intermittently with Rachel, joined her in Tiwaeno. Catherine was working toward her Ph.D. in linguistics at Indiana University; her analysis of Auca grammar was to be her thesis. This research would form the structural backup for Rachel's translation of the Scriptures into the Auca language.

Kimo, once he was convinced that God had truly spoken through His Carving which was being taught and translated, matured steadily in his knowledge of God. "Old things" had quite literally "passed away," and he very naturally assumed leadership in the growing Auca church. Under his thatched roof informal gatherings continued to be held for reading the Gospel of Mark as it was being translated, and for talking to God. Very early each Sunday, God's day, there were special meetings. Each Sunday evening a "sunset Sunday school" was conducted by Dyuwi for the children. So eager was Gikita to learn more of God that he often slipped in quietly to the children's meetings to hear Dyuwi's Bible stories.

Concern for the young men growing up in Tiwaeno led Kimo to encourage them openly to believe in Jesus, to follow His trail to heaven.

One Sunday morning Dayuma was urging them to voice their decision. One of them, Toña, who was leaning on the bamboo fence around Kimo's house where the meeting was held, spoke up spontaneously. He said that he wanted Jesus' blood to wash his heart. Under Kimo's teaching and influence, Toña grew in his knowledge of God's Carving. Early hostility toward foreign-

ers was transformed into strong desire to learn more of the
word they had brought.

Dawa's strong faith had inspired Kimo from the day the Gospel entered Tiwaeno.

"I was the first one to believe in Jesus' name after Dayuma
came," Dawa once said. " 'I am always going to believe in Jesus,'
I decided.

"Then Nimu came, and she said, 'This is what it says in God's
Carving.' So I thought to myself, 'It is true.' Who of the ancestors spoke the truth like this? They just spoke wild. This foreigner is speaking the truth. Did the ancestors say that after you
died you would be raised again? I always will believe in Jesus.
And then, having died, I surely will not die again. Once dying,
then in the heavens without dying I will live.' This is what I
thought.

"Then the others said,'The foreigners will shoot us with their
guns. We must all flee.' I said, 'Why do we flee?' Always I want
to believe in God."

One by one the Tiwaeno dwellers began to accept the words
from God's Carving as more dependable than those of the
ancestors.

When Kimo's house became too crowded, he suggested that
a larger thatched hut for God's-speaking-house be erected. He
decided that it should be built high off the ground with a hardwood palm platform to prevent the intrusion of the imported
geese and nosy goats which roamed the Tiwaeno clearing.

To Rachel's surprise, she found upon her return from a trip
to Quito that the building was all finished, complete with a
notched pole by which the worshipers could ascend. The Aucas
still preferred to shinny up the big poles at the corners.

As their knowledge of God's Carving grew, so too did their
concern for the downriver enemy relatives. Recently, there
had been news of the spearing of two Quichuas and the capture
of a small girl on Father River. Only a day's journey from Tiwa-

eno the group had seen the footprints of downriver Aucas. This could mean a surprise attack in Tiwaeno.

The Auca Christians prayed for their relatives, asking God for some way to reach them. But how could one live if he went to them? They would only spear him, some said. The risk would be great.

Before the meeting in God's-speaking-house had begun on that memorable Sunday morning in November, 1963, Dyuwi said to Rachel, "Nimu, I have something to tell you . . . But I will wait until after we sing."

Following the first song, Dyuwi said to the group, "Last night I dreamed that God told me to go to the downriver people!" His face was beaming.

"If you go, you will only be killed!" someone cried out. All of the Aucas began to talk at once of the difficulties, of the snake-infested trail, and of the probability of being speared. No one knew this better than Dyuwi.

"It is God who sends me and I will go," he said. "If I die, my body will be buried, and my soul will go to God's house. Then God will send someone else to them as He sent someone else to us after we speared the foreigners."

In successive days God spoke again to Dyuwi:

" 'Everywhere, in every land, I exist,' like that God spoke to me. 'Go to the downriver Aucas and I will work for you. I am One who exists everywhere.' "

Recalling verses from the Gospel of Mark, Dyuwi said,

"Two by two, two by two, we should go. Do you understand?

"What others will You in turn speak to like that?" Dyuwi in the Auca way of addressing God was asking for volunteers to go with him.

Gikita, moved by Dyuwi's words, prayed aloud at the end of

the meeting, "God, You are everywhere, and if You say, 'Yes, you go,' I too will go to the downriver group. But You go first, and I will follow. And if You say, 'No,' I will stay at home. Lord, I was old before I ever knew God's Carving."

# 3 ❧ "I HEARD THE FOREIGNERS HAD SHOT YOU"

"Let's ask God to send us someone from the downriver group to open the way," Rachel suggested as the Auca Christians discussed the dangers of the contact. She reminded them that Dayuma had fled to the *outside*. In every gathering there was fervent prayer to God for a safe meeting with the downriver enemies *without bloodshed.*

Wycliffe's pilots shared the concern for contact with enemy Aucas, knowing that they might furnish air cover for a ground party. They had long followed the established pattern of flying the Napo River route and then heading sharply into Tiwaeno, rather than taking the shorter route that involved flying directly over enemy territory. On occasion the pilots had seen naked Aucas on the ground, their spears pointed threateningly at the plane. Recently, the pilots had heard of Aucas spearing on the Napo River not far from Limoncocha. At several points on the river boundary Aucas had speared Quichua Indians as well as other foreigners who were fishing, or were traveling on the Aucas' side. One Quichua had been found with seventeen spears still in his body.

Merrill Piper, a JAARS pilot who had flown to the jungle hacienda where Rachel lived in 1955 and had met Dayuma, joined efforts to reach her people. He now began flights over downriver Auca territory in search of clearings visible from the air and to look for Auca houses. Several were spotted.

In January, 1964, he flew some of the Aucas from Tiwaeno to Limoncocha for medical attention at Wycliffe's clinic. While there they heard from Ecuadorians that some of their downriver relatives had recently attacked foreigners living on Father

River. Learning also that outsiders were boldly crossing into Auca territory, they became concerned; more would be killed if this practice continued.

When Dabu, Kimo's older brother from Tiwaeno, heard the story he said, "If outsiders had come into our territory a few years ago, we would have killed them." He then warned *all* outsiders to keep out of downriver Auca territory. "The downriver relatives still kill outsiders. We used to kill that way," he added.

In February a large official gathering was held at Limoncocha where representatives of all the Indian tribes of Ecuador performed in colorful dances and song. The Aucas on that occasion asked the government for a permanent area to be formally recognized and delineated on the map of the country. They were eager to have the "lines carved on the paper," guaranteeing them their land. Dayuma had previously offered her cooperation in bringing all the Aucas in to the Tiwaeno area, thus opening the remainder of the jungle for commerce. Dyuwi, the chorister of the Auca church, had composed his first hymn as a prayer concerning their land:

> Lord, You give us our land,
> and here happily serving You
> we will live.

Merrill, who took Gikita, Dyuwi, and the latter's young nephew, Kinta, to Limoncocha for the big celebration, flew them over downriver territory. He wanted to take advantage of the Aucas' sharp eyes for spotting small clearings and houses. Kinta, who was young and had no holes in his earlobes, sat directly behind Merrill. Gikita and Dyuwi sat on the opposite side in the small plane, peering down eagerly.

Suddenly, there was an outburst of Auca exclamations that Merrill could not understand. But there was no mistaking the wild gestures: houses *down there!* Merrill flew the plane lower and slower. Sure enough! A small clearing was plainly visible.

For a still better view he circled around and flew over the clearing in the opposite direction until they were directly over the tiny opening in the forest floor. Kinta's keen eyes saw a naked downriver Auca streak across the clearing at the roar of the plane. Gikita and Dyuwi on their side saw others sprint in fright toward the low door of the long houses thatched down to the ground.

They were having their *first sight* of their downriver relatives in many years!

When they returned to Tiwaeno, there was a lively report of the trip. The excitement of seeing other jungle Indians at Limoncocha was eclipsed by the sighting of Auca life in the downriver wilderness. Gikita's last experience there had been a spearing raid years before. Now, as a believer, he was praying for a chance to meet his wild relatives in peace.

Plans for traveling to the spot near Father River were discussed in Tiwaeno. On what rivers could they travel? Where was the trail? How could they be received in peace? Who was still living there in that clearing? Was Niwa alive? Day after day, and at night as they swung in their hammocks around the fires, the Auca Christians talked with one another and with God about how to attempt a contact.

Few shared Rachel's faith that God would bring someone *out* from the group as He had led Dayuma out from Tiwaeno. In May when she and Catherine made a trip to Quito, there was still no firm plan for going downriver.

One day routine radio business from Wycliffe's jungle base at Limoncocha was interrupted for an emergency message for Rachel, still in Quito. A wounded Auca girl had been found on the Napo River and was seriously ill in a remote jungle settlement. Could Rachel fly immediately to see her?

Bad flying weather prevented Rachel from reaching the settlement until three days later. The girl was still gravely ill. Frightened, her face flushed with fever, she lay suffering in the foreigner's house. Huge balsa earplugs and bangs cut back over her ears identified her with the downriver group.

The girl glared at Rachel in obvious anger and turned her face. *Another* foreigner! Her face reflected hatred for all the strange world around her. She was alone and badly wounded; the foreigners' metal was still wedged in her thigh. She refused to eat. No one in the small settlement could speak her language.

"Who are you?" Rachel asked in Auca.

"I am empty-named!" was the retort. In Auca that meant *None of your business!*

Rachel continued to speak to the girl in her own language: "I heard the foreigners had shot you. I came to help you, and to talk with you . . ."

Suddenly, the girl realized that she was understanding the words this foreigner was speaking.

"Who are *you?*" she asked Rachel.

"My name is Nimu—"

Nimu! The name of her aunt who had been killed by outsiders! The girl quickly sat up, looked straight at the foreign woman, and asked in a strong voice, "Are *you* an *Auca?*"

"No, but I live with the Aucas, and I am like a sister to Dayuma," Rachel said. "We both live with the 'dear ones,' the Aucas who live upriver, far from here. I came to help you, because I heard you were sick. We live in peace, we live very happily . . . Who are you?"

"I am Oncaye," said the patient. And she slumped back on the bed.

Soon she was talking freely, giving the names of her parents, her brothers, her sisters, and of prime importance to Auca kinship, the names of her grandparents. The names were familiar to Rachel, for she had spent hours memorizing all the names and relationships the Tiwaeno Aucas could recall. This information would be helpful in establishing peaceful contact with the downriver relatives. The wounded girl was closely related to

Aucas who had fled earlier from her group and now lived in Tiwaeno. She was also related to Dayuma.

"I live with your four sisters and your brother-in-law upriver. We all live with Dayuma in Gikita's group," Rachel told her.

"My grandmother told me Dayuma was killed long ago by the Eaters-of-people," Oncaye said in a quiet voice. She was too weak to talk more. Closing her eyes, she fell into a deep sleep.

Oncaye awoke in a stranger world, in a different house. There were no jungle trees around her, no Father River in sight. She was frightened and sick and in agonizing pain. She groaned, and covered her face with the sheet.

Then she heard someone speaking in her own language—or was she dreaming? No—there was the voice again, and somehow it was familiar.

"Oncaye, it is I . . . Gakamo, your sister!"

The young patient who had been flown out of the jungle to a hospital in Shell Mera finally peeped out from under the sheet. She saw her sister, much older now and wearing clothes.

"I have come to be near you, Oncaye," Gakamo said. "And here is Dawa, our relative who came from downriver. She lives in Gikita's group. We want you to get better and come home with us."

It seemed like a dream, but there was Gakamo standing by her bed. Yes, it was Gakamo, who had fled upriver many years ago!

Oncaye thrust out a trembling hand and grasped Gakamo's.

"Don't leave me, Gakamo, don't leave me!" she sobbed, clinging to her sister in desperation.

Gakamo held her hand and spoke to her reassuringly. As her crying subsided, Oncaye said in a steadier voice, "My mother, Titada, told me to come and get her if I lived well on the outside. If I don't return, my brothers will go again and spear foreigners on the Big River."

"We will ask God to make you better—"

"Is God still *alive?*" Oncaye asked in amazement.

"Yes. God never dies," Gakamo replied. "Believing in Him, we will live forever. Dayuma came back from living a long time with the foreigners, and she taught us about Father God—"

"I thought Dayuma was eaten by the foreigners long ago. Is that why the foreigners hit me with their fire, to *eat* me?"

"No, little sister . . . Later, seeing that you are better, we will teach you more. When tomorrow comes they will take the metal out of your leg."

Gakamo and Dawa leaned over Oncaye, their long black hair hanging down as a screen. The three talked softly, exchanging secrets that only Aucas would understand.

Gakamo then offered Oncaye a bowl of banana drink.

"Little sister," she said, "having drunk your banana drink, sleep!"

# 4 ❦ NEW WORLD UPRIVER

After the bullet had been removed from Oncaye's thigh she began to improve rapidly. Gakamo brought her *real Auca* food. The foreigners' food, flavored with salt and "hot stuff" unfamiliar to Aucas, had nauseated her.

Gakamo was constantly by her sister's side, briefing her on the new way of life in Tiwaeno. Oncaye in turn told her of their grandmother's brutal murder, and of finding Aunt Nimu's decaying remains on the banks of Father River.

"Our brothers are planning to spear *again*," Oncaye told Gakamo.

As the sisters talked, Dawa listened hungrily for word about her family. It had been many years since she learned anything about her brothers. Were any of them still alive? Oncaye knew only that they had fled to another part of the forest long, long ago.

Gakamo told Oncaye that their other sisters, Boika—named for her grandmother—Wiba, and Ompoda, were in Tiwaeno and waiting to see her. "Now loving God we live," Gakamo said. "Spearing and fleeing no more, we live in peace. We have thrown out the teachings of the witch-doctors."

This change amazed Oncaye, who all her life had feared devils and the cures of the witch-doctor. Even in the hospital she had feared that the devils would come and suck her blood.

*Did Niwa still live?* Gakamo wanted to know.

Yes, but he was old and sickly. Recently, a tree had fallen on him, leaving him crippled. He would surely die soon unless someone could help him.

As Rachel assisted in caring for Oncaye, she heard stories of the downriver group, and was reminded of the early days of contact with Dayuma when she had first learned of Auca brutality. From Shell Mera she wrote on May 28, 1964: "The young girl could be the key to the whole downriver situation, if the Lord works it out as He did for Dayuma. We must wait and watch and pray to see God's plan. . . . " She remembered her prayer that God would bring someone *out* from the downriver group.

Oncaye wanted to know more about Rachel, the white foreigner with blue eyes. And how was it that she was called Nimu? She had been surprised to hear the name of her aunt at the outsiders' house where Rachel met her. Now there was a new Nimu in the Auca family!

Finally, the happy day arrived for Oncaye's release from the hospital and official approval for her to fly in the Wycliffe plane to Tiwaeno. On this flight she was awake and alert and straining to see the contour of every ridge, the twist of every river. Her guides Gakamo and Dawa gave an animated commentary on this new land, the features of which differed from the deep downriver forests where she had grown up.

Landing at the Tiwaeno airfield, she saw for the first time a large group of Auca thatched houses right out in the open at one end of the field. And there were more Aucas than she had ever seen in her life, older Aucas and children wearing foreigners' clothing. Some wore shorts, others only shirts, but everyone wore *something*. Empty earholes, which once held balsa plugs, proved they were *Aucas!*

During her first days in Tiwaeno many of the Aucas visited Oncaye's bedside in Nimu's house. Auca spearings over a period of almost eight years since the last contact were recalled. Oncaye was told that when Dayuma had first returned from the outside, Gikita and the other Tiwaeno men were prepared to go downriver to spear again. But God's Carving had come, and life was different in the upriver group. Gikita was now asking God for a way to share the good news with his former enemies.

When, upon Oncaye's arrival, he had heard of old Niwa's plight, he prayed, "Lord, how can we get medicine to him so he will be able to hear God's Carving before he dies?"

Oncaye and her sisters wept at recollections of bloody feuding and of other brutalities. But big sister Boika explained to Oncaye that "loving the Lord, we no longer bury our babies alive!"

And they recalled with hilarity pleasant childhood days, spent in climbing tall trees to gather wild fruit or racing through the forest on a wild pig hunt.

One day Oncaye, who was now readily eating foods she had never before tasted, refused to swallow a red capsule of prescribed medicine. Rachel exhausted her Auca vocabulary, to no avail. She finally called Gikita; his authority might help. To Rachel's surprise he began abruptly to lecture the girl about the witch-doctor and magic cures. These were of the devil and were not used in Tiwaeno, he declared firmly. "Believing in God, we pray only to Him—and take the medicine that Nimu gives us." Oncaye had associated the red capsule with magic cures used by the witch-doctor and would not take it from Rachel. Gikita's explanation was convincing; the capsule was swallowed with no further objection.

Also during Oncaye's convalescence there were long hours of planning for the trip downriver when she would bring her mother to Tiwaeno. She continued to live with Rachel, whose loving care and concern had won her complete loyalty.

"You are just like my mother, and this is like my home," she told Rachel. Responding to the hymns and stories from God's Carving, she joined the others in memorizing Bible verses. She was bright and learned quickly. Although still weak, she joined the early morning reading class that Rachel taught, anxious to read God's Carving for *herself*.

As the downriver trip neared, Dyuwi and the other Christians suggested the possibility of the "wood-bee's" flying overhead to guide them, and to drop provisions if need arose.

Oncaye told her Tiwaeno family of the Things that had flown over her clearing. One day high in a tree she had seen one buzzing just over her head. "Who and who were in that Thing?" she wanted to know.

"That was Gikita and Dyuwi and Kinta!" they all agreed when the facts were compared. "We were looking for your people that day!" Gikita declared, remembering well the small clearing and the first glimpse of downriver people since he had last gone to spear. Gesturing excitedly, Gikita showed Oncaye how the "wood-bee" had buzzed low over the small clearing, then circled around and flew over it again when people were spotted on the ground.

"It was *you* and *Dyuwi* I saw that day! I saw the holes in your ears!" Oncaye exclaimed, her body trembling with joy at the memory of what she had seen from the treetop the day she recovered the monkey. She hadn't been talking "wild"! How she longed to return and tell her family all she was hearing!

Oncaye learned that it was now the custom to talk to God about all things great and small. By November she was praying to God at the table, thanking Him for the food. Rachel wrote in a letter: "This morning Oncaye prayed that Kimo, who had gone hunting, would get a tapir so that there would be 'a little bit' of food for all. Before noon Kimo was back with a tapir, and all who were free went to the river where they were butchering it to get big chunks of meat for their families. It was encouraging for one who did not know of Him a few months ago."

There had been much prayer about the downriver trip. By February, 1965, a small band of Auca missionaries were ready to go. Uncertainties continued to plague them. Catherine Peeke wrote of the plans:

"Now the chonta is ripe, that rich palm fruit which marks for the jungle Indian 'another year' and insures for the traveler an abundant supply along his unmarked way. Oncaye feels the urgency that with the passing of the moon all the chonta will be gone, rains will begin again, rivers will be swollen, and travel will become increasingly more difficult.

"Oncaye swings in her hammock and softly sings to herself the songs of home as the day draws near. Afraid? Won't they spear? *Not if we talk to God about it!* says this young Auca maiden who had not even heard of the Christians' God at chonta season last year. Last night at a special prayer meeting concerning her trip back home she ventured to pray aloud (not very loud) in the presence of all the young men and women who had gathered to pray—quite a victory for her!"

There was animated discussion as to who would go. Dyuwi wanted to go, for God had spoken directly to him. In the review of family relationships it was discovered that he and Oncaye were close relatives; they could travel together, but who would go with them? Toña wanted to go, but his mother had objected; scenes of family spearings were still too vividly remembered. Another woman should go along with Oncaye, and someone was needed to guide them.

"Oncaye just listens to all this speculation about who will go, or whom the Lord will lead," Catherine continued. "For her, it seems to be immaterial, for she's going home, and God is going with her, and what difference does it make if she travels alone?"

On the day of departure Dyuwi set out, followed closely by Toña, whose mother had finally given consent. Rachel had selected a few necessary medicines, including snakebite serum. Dyuwi carried a small pack on his back and a bush knife in his hand. As he left his wife, Oba, and his small children, he prayed, "Lord, You guard my family."

Oncaye called to her white puppy and followed the two men. It had been decided that her half-sister, Boika, should accompany her, since she was perhaps the most qualified to serve as a guide. Boika and her husband, Monga, had fled most recently toward Tiwaeno along this route. Boika left her baby with relatives. Her older children had told her, "You go alone, Mother.

If both of you are speared, we will cry a lot. If you are speared and go to heaven, dying, we will see you again."

Catherine and Rachel prayed that evening for the missionary party who would spend the first night on the banks of Fish River. They were concerned for Oncaye, who appeared fragile for the rigors of a trip that would cover one hundred miles of unmarked jungle. Her bullet wounds had not completely healed, and she had just recovered from a bout with the flu, a result of her contact with outsiders' ailments.

Oncaye had confirmed the intentions of her family group to locate Gikita's group upriver and spear in retaliation for previous killings. Would Dyuwi's group now meet them coming upriver?

Also, just before the group left Tiwaeno, word had come of a skirmish with outsiders in which an Auca had been killed. Would the downriver relatives be in a furious mood when the band from upriver arrived at Oncaye's family clearing?

Dayuma and Komi left two days later to wait at an intermediate point on the trail to receive the downriver people who would be returning with the missionary party. Rachel kept baby Nancy, which freed Dayuma for easier foot travel and for fleeing, if necessary. Apprehensive but hopeful, Rachel and Catherine continued to pray for the Auca friends on trek.

On the evening of the third day Rachel was walking on the airstrip and carrying baby Nancy when she heard someone call, "Dyuwi has returned!" She turned around to see a very serious-looking Dyuwi, pack on his back—and alone.

"Where are the others?" Rachel asked, fearing that they had been killed.

"They are close by," came the welcome answer. "Oncaye's wounds hurt lots and lots!"

Soon the other straggled in, tired and disheartened. They had lost the trail and circled back to the same spot. Boika could not remember the trail; it had been many years since she fled upriver. A tree had fallen, hitting Dyuwi and hurting Toña's knee. They had talked "lots and lots" to Father God, telling Him how much they wanted to reach their downriver family. Finally, they were forced to turn back.

In the days that followed, Dyuwi talked much to God as some of the group tried to dissuade him from a second attempt.

*Lord, You told me to go the first time, now what do You say?*

Assured of his call, he was eager to obey. He planned for another trip a few weeks later.

A second expedition ventured out, joined by Gikita and Minkayi, who offered to cut the trail with machetes. Three of the Palm Beach killers led by Dyuwi, the youngest of them, were now risking their lives to reach their savage relatives with the Gospel.

"Lord, You Yourself do it!" Dayuma prayed, using a strong Auca reflexive pronoun as she committed the valiant band to God.

The Tiwaeno group waited and prayed, too preoccupied to concentrate fully on tasks at hand. Komi found it difficult to sit long at his reading lessons while his father, Gikita, faced contact with killers downriver.

Six endless days of silence were broken by a shout coming from the edge of the Tiwaeno clearing. A handful of weary travelers emerged, single file.

*What happened?* everyone wanted to know.

They had tried many trails, but were always blocked. The rainy season that had begun early left the large rivers impassable.

That night a weary, subdued group of Aucas sat by the fires, resting and thinking and talking in quiet tones. Some of the group said, *I told you so!* but others concluded *Talking to God, we will go again.*

Dyuwi lay in his hammock and talked to God. Again and again God told him to go, and not to be discouraged. Dyuwi knew that he would look again for the trail when the rainy season ended.

# 5 ❦ BAPTISM ON "PALM BEACH"

Dyuwi's call to take God's Carving to his people involved learning to *read* it. Following odd squiggles on the page was a difficult art for rugged Indians to master. But Dyuwi was determined to read the pages of the Gospel of Mark, which Rachel was typing as she translated. The delay in the downriver contact gave him more time to increase his reading ability.

Early in 1965 the Gospel of Mark was finally published. There would be a jubilant Easter dedication. And Dyuwi could take this first precious portion of God's Carving on the next trip.

❦ The translation of Mark had been a long uphill climb. The arduous hours at the hacienda when Dayuma began slowly to recall the language she had purposely forgotten had finally resulted in the Auca alphabet, the first time the language had ever been "carved"! Then followed painstaking research for the grammatical rules of a language never before spoken by any outsider. Added to unique syntactic forms were exotic semantic collocations, such as "he was buried, then he died"—referring to Aucas who were buried alive. Auca narrations had another frequent phrase, "spearing and fleeing."

Catherine Peeke wrote of the difficulties in translating abstract concepts, a special challenge to Rachel and Dayuma: "There are deficiencies in vocabulary because the Aucas have apparently lived without any cognizance of what the civilized world about them is doing. In this category lie the concepts of buying and selling, or even of trading; any form of specialized labor, as a carpenter, fisherman, teacher, sower; any religious or governmental organization, any concept of village or city; any idea of law, trial, or authority. They know neither bread nor paper so used their term for 'wasp's nest' for both. 'Wasp's nest food' is differentiated from 'wasp's nest which is given-taken' (money). Coins are 'metal fish scales.'

"They do not know horses, donkeys, or cattle, and have never seen grapevines. They do not use grinding stones nor know of stones used in building. Market places and political boundaries are unknown to them. They know no servant-master relationship, no rich, no poor. Teaching-learning situations are not recognized.

"The fact that Dayuma has had experience in the outside world and understands something of the political, economic, educational, and religious systems of her own country alleviates the situation quite drastically."

"Disciple" was rendered "one who lives following Jesus." "Scribe," "teacher," "priest," and "prophet" were expressed by an Auca form, "one who customarily performs a certain function." But "one who customarily teaches" became "one who teaches that they may hear," because in Auca the concept included the *learner.*

The notion of Jesus' commanding the wind and the waves to cease their turmoil was rendered in Auca: "Jesus then said, 'Why *ever* does the wind blow, for goodness' sake!' Then it became not blowing. 'Water, quiet down, don't do it!' He said. Then the water quickly quieted down and it was not doing anything."

The Gospel of Mark was approved by Wycliffe consultants for publication by the American Bible Society, thus crowning nine years of linguistic labor.

"For Dayuma and me it represents the end of a long tedious job—toil, sweat, and tears," Rachel remembers. As the brief prayer of thanksgiving was voiced at Limoncocha base where the final approval was given, Rachel sensed a surge of emotion

too private to share. "And I headed for a lovely jungle trail," she
continues, "for how would Dayuma and the other Aucas understand that these tears were different?"

At last the precious cargo of God's Carving reached
Tiwaeno. "Before the plane landed," Rachel wrote, "Dyuwi
expressed the feelings of us all by yodeling in the Auca way a
great big joyful *'Uuuooo'* that echoed around the banks of the
Tiwaeno!" And the Aucas buzzed with excitement when the
first package of books was opened and they saw the beautifully
illustrated copies of Mark.

Special guests arrived for the dedication. Wycliffe's Ecuador
Director, Don Johnson, and his wife, Helen, accompanied Steve
and Phil Saint, sons of Nate and Marj Saint, in the JAARS plane.
Steve, now fourteen years of age and living with his mother in
Quito, had visited his Aunt Rachel in Tiwaeno several times
before.

The Aucas affectionately held the new books and read from
them during the service.

"Oncaye's copy trembled in her hand from sheer joy and
excitement!" Rachel wrote her mother, who had prayed for this
day of triumph. One by one Auca pupils each read a verse of
the resurrection story from Mark. Oncaye beamed as she confi-
dently read her verse concerning Mary Magdalene "who before
had seven devils, but they were all cast out!" Hadn't she, too,
been freed from fear of the devils? Oncaye could know the
meaning of the words.

Many of the other Aucas seated on the palm bark floor of the
thatched chapel had also experienced release from the crippling power of demons and the tyranny of fear. What a day of
rejoicing for redeemed killers who were celebrating Satan's
defeat in their midst!

They chanted simple hymns of praise to Christ, happy to be

rid of the witch-doctor's chants to the demons. The demons came with the use of the witch-doctor's potent drugs and asked, *Whom shall we curse that he may die?* Never again would they fear the magic jaguar, sent to pounce on them or to steal their soul. In the form of a fish, a doomed person's spirit was smoked and eaten at the river—and in three days the person died, chanting the same song as the witch-doctor, far away in another part of the forest. Many Aucas had died that way!

But Jesus was greater than all the demons! He commanded them to leave and never return. The witch-doctor could not do that. Demons would always return and speak deep in the throat, without the moving of human lips.

God's Carving had broken the power of the spear in Tiwaeno. At last the good life sought by the ancestors had been found again. The ancestors said that an old Auca woman had once become young again because of a magic dart holder. Through its use manioc also appeared in full bloom, and banana trees suddenly bore fruit! But some evil ancestor had misused the magic holder and its power was lost.

Now through God's Carving the Aucas knew a loving, powerful Father who had destroyed death and gave new bodies. Their old bodies would be discarded like old fishing shacks, but they would have new bodies when Jesus came to call them.

The words of God's Carving were powerful and clear. Dayuma could not conceal her pleasure after the long years of work; the reward was sweet! She whispered to Rachel, "I have just read a page and a half . . . it is 'out in the open' . . . very clear!"

To the delight of his Indian friends, Steve Saint, who had learned some Auca on his earlier trips, read his verse in turn. Young Phil sat cuddled beside Kimo, who was "thrilled beyond all telling" with the new book. When he had difficulty reading his verse, Phil coached him quietly.There were some in the gathering that morning who were mindful of the miracle in action: sons of one of the Palm Beach martyrs were worshiping in peace with their father's killers!

And the thatched chapel built by the Palm Beach killers was being extended at both ends to accommodate the downriver relatives who would be brought to hear God's Carving.

At the close of the meeting Kimo prayed in moving words: "Father God, You are alive. This is Your day and all of us have come to worship You. They brought us copies of Your Carving, enough for everybody. We accept it, saying, 'This is the truth.' We want all of Your Carving.

"Father, we live here wondering about death. You know all things, so when You say, 'That's enough!' we will die and go to heaven. But if you say we will not die, then we'll keep on believing until Jesus comes and calls. But how could the unbelievers follow when He calls? It's impossible. Those who want to take a second wife—it is the devil who is trying to get them to do that.

"Our hearts are clean because Jesus' blood dripped down from the cross and washed us. The cross is like a tree chopped down to bridge a ravine. Jesus, You are our trail to heaven. You alone are our Chief. I have finished speaking."

The promise of Christ's second coming had often caused Kimo to wonder how soon He would appear in the sky. One night as he was in the jungle alone downstream, where he was building a canoe by day, he thought Jesus had come:

"It was a dark night, but I hadn't yet gone to sleep when suddenly there was a brilliant light in the sky and the place burst into light! It was brighter than day and all the trees around me became very, very white!

"I was startled and thought, 'Who has ever seen a light like that before?' Then I thought, 'What does God's Carving say? "Long, long ago Jesus went into the heavens, and suddenly returning He will come." This must be it.' I was overcome with joy and just waited for the shout! Then it disappeared, and I was left alone in the pitch blackness of the night.

" 'When will Jesus come back?' I thought. Suddenly, just like that, He will come. Now I understand. I just stayed on there talking to the Lord a long time. He seemed so near! I said to myself, 'If Nimu saw this, she undoubtedly cried out, *"Badogaa* —Hail to the coming One!" ' "

"Marvelous meteor!" Rachel had commented. "And more marvelous the light that has shone into Auca lives as they have begun to read God's Carving!"

Following the dedication of the Gospel of Mark, plans were made for Steve to spend part of the summer in Tiwaeno. He liked to hunt and fish with his Auca friends.

Steve's sister, Kathy, almost sixteen, wrote Rachel of her desire to be baptized by Auca believers. Steve, upon hearing of her decision, said that he "would like to show my faith as a Christian by being baptized by the Aucas." When his mother learned of the plans, she suggested that the entire family visit Palm Beach where Nate Saint and his friends were killed.

The family joined Steve in Tiwaeno. It was decided to visit the beach first and to have the baptismal service upon their return. The party set out for the Curaray. Kimo and Dyuwi led the way on a beautiful jungle trail festooned with flowering vines and gigantic feathery ferns.

The Saint children bounded ahead with the Indians, laughing and shouting Auca phrases. Dayuma, who knew some Spanish, conversed with Marj Saint. Rachel was delighted to be traveling with members of her brother's family.

At the Curaray the group boarded canoes for Palm Beach. They poled downstream until mid-afternoon when a downpour drove them to shelter, fortunately at a spot on the river where Gikita had previously built fishing shacks. There they found dry wood for a fire and made coffee. When the rain ended they continued toward Palm Beach.

"Late in the afternoon," Steve remembers, "we rounded a normal-looking bend in the river to behold what Kimo solemnly pointed out to be Palm Beach. I felt rather let down. The beach wasn't as big or as sandy as pictures showed it to have been when my Dad was there."

Steve's reaction to the beach echoed Dawa's thoughts upon having seen a photograph of it one day in Rachel's house in Tiwaeno. *It must have been in God's plan. That beach has never been like that —long and level—before or since.*

Dawa had witnessed the massacre of the missionaries in 1956. She watched Dayuma's mother, Akawo, distract the foreigners as Gikita and the younger killers prepared to attack. Two other women, Mintaka and Miñi, aided in the deception.

One by one the foreigners had fallen. Although they fired shots into the air, warning the Aucas that they had means of defense, they chose to be killed by Auca spears.

Deep remorse had followed when through Dayuma the Aucas learned that the foreigners had come in peace, desiring to bring them God's Carving. This knowledge was received too late to save the lives of Jim Elliot and Roger Youderian, Pete Fleming and Ed McCulley—and Nate Saint, Nimu's brother—all "good" foreigners who wanted only to help the Aucas.

"Yes," Dawa had told Rachel, "I'm sure they tried to tell Mintaka about God. They pointed up to heaven and said 'Father,' then they pointed to earth."

Meditating sadly for a moment on the death of the men as she looked at the photograph, Dawa had suddenly brightened and said, "Dying we will see them again, and seeing them, we will be happy."

Now nine years later, Dawa and her husband, Kimo, were at Palm Beach again, together with Nate's widow, Marj, and her three children. Kimo's concern for their comfort was a touching indication of transformed life. He and Dyuwi made palm-leaf shelters for the night, and spread large leaves on the jungle floor for beds. Through the night the Auca men watched the rain-swollen river rise to a dangerous height, and alerted the group to move to higher ground.

Before retiring, Marj had asked if the baptismal service could be held on the beach at dawn, as time would be short when they returned to Tiwaeno for the flight back to Quito. Kimo and Dyuwi had consented, and the service was arranged.

Oncaye had also expressed a desire to be baptized. She told Rachel that she would like to be "entered into the water," that she "loved the Lord *very* much." Iniwa, Dayuma's foster brother who came on the trip, also wanted to participate.

The group gathered at dawn. Kimo talked to the four teenagers about the meaning of baptism, the need to leave sin and to live truly for God. They then sang an Auca hymn, and Dayuma read the verses concerning baptism from the first chapter of Mark.

Kathy was the first to be baptized by Kimo and Dyuwi, who immersed her in the Curaray. Oncaye was next, and then Steve, followed by Iniwa.

Closing the ceremony, Kimo prayed, "Lord, long ago, not knowing You, we sinned *right here.* Now, believing in You, we are going to meet You in the air!"

Kimo and Dyuwi then led the group from the beach down a short jungle trail to the site of the missionaries' graves.

Marj and Rachel had circled over the scene of death in 1956. The other four widows were also in the U.S. Army plane on that sad occasion.

Two of the Palm Beach killers now stood by the graves with Marj and Rachel. Canopied by a luxurious leafy ceiling, the group sang in the silent forest the hymn the five men and their families had sung just before leaving for Palm Beach the last time:

> We rest on Thee, our Shield and our Defender,
> Thine is the battle, Thine shall be the praise;
> When passing through the gates of pearly splendor,
> Victors, we rest with Thee through endless days.

"Tears held back for years flowed freely, at least for the Saint family," Rachel recorded later. "As I looked up, after prayer, I saw above the graves five red jungle flowers, standing straight and tall, with the sun filtering through that gorgeous forest!"

When the group moved onto the sunlit beach, Kimo showed Rachel where the "ancestor's trail," the main route from downriver, crossed the Curaray on Palm Beach. "If the men hadn't landed on *that* beach," her record continued, "they might never have had the contact that led eventually to reaching the Aucas." The Indians again emphasized the fact that at the time of the massacre it had been high, dry, and level, and twice as long. Now it was half under water, impossible as a landing strip.

Upon returning to Tiwaeno, Rachel reflected: "It was sheer joy to go to Palm Beach with Aucas whose hearts were as moved as ours by the miracle of their changed lives."

# 6 ❦ "PUT DOWN YOUR SPEARS!"

Early in February, 1966, pilot Don Smith located a small group of houses downriver, some distance from those spotted previously. The fleeing Aucas, realizing that they had been seen, had made a new hideout.

In Tiwaeno, Dayuma, Dyuwi, and Oncaye were selected for an overflight with Don. Heading eastward, they flew over the green sea of trees, a flat expanse with no distinguishing features. Almost immediately Don located the new houses, something he said he could not do but "once in five hundred times."

With the late afternoon sun striking clearly against the houses, Oncaye, looking down, was able to identify her mother, even though both men and women had long flowing black hair. She recognized another of Niwa's wives with her many children, the youngest being carried in a bark-cloth sling. Frightened by the roar of the plane, she quickly shooed her big flock of naked children toward an open doorway. A muscular man holding several spears came to the middle of the clearing and made angry gestures at the plane. Other terrified Aucas watched the plane as they remained half-hidden by trees.

After the flight there was serious discussion in Tiwaeno regarding another overland trip to the houses. Dyuwi decided that the relatives should be given time to "cool off." He busied himself by repairing his leaking thatched roof to insure comfort for his wife, Oba, and their four small children, since the rainy season was about due.

As Dyuwi worked on his house, he was filled with doubts. *I have lots of little children . . . how can I go?* But he was finally convinced that God wanted him to go. *Lord, I will obey You, and go.*

A portable two-way radio had been conditioned for the ground party, for contact with Tiwaeno and Limoncocha. Dan Choisser, who with his wife, Ruth, faithfully operated the JAARS radio transmitter at Limoncocha, came to Tiwaeno with Don Smith to instruct the travelers in its use. Toña, who would be a member of the expedition, attempted a practice call. He shook with fright and was unable to talk. With Don Smith's sympathetic reassurance and a little more practice, Toña became confident. Maps were studied, and the route downriver agreed upon.

In mid-February Dyuwi and Toña, Oncaye and Boika, set out once again. They had a small amount of food, medicine, and the radio for emergency calls to Tiwaeno or Limoncocha. Don Smith would fly over them every other day to guide them toward their destination.

Some days later there was a radio call from the party: they had found *footprints* of Oncaye's family and were following them. Two days later, another message. Through the static, four names were heard clearly, those of Oncaye's mother, of two of her brothers, and of Dyuwi's foster sister. Hopes soared in Tiwaeno as Dayuma asked, "Will they come to Tiwaeno with you?" The answer was a heavy blow: "They are all speared—*dead!* We must flee in the night!"

Several anxious days passed with no further radio message. Finally, Dayuma's husband, Komi, with Kimo and Dawa, left at dawn for Fish River, praying that they would find the party, who would be traveling in that direction. The following morning Komi came running back to Tiwaeno, very excited, perspiring, and shouting, "The downriver people are on the trail, coming to spear!"

Shortly, others of the two groups began to arrive. Toña was limping from sore, swollen feet. They all dropped into their hammocks.

Ten grueling days had passed since the first group left Tiwaeno. Toña had made a map of their wanderings downriver. On
it the battle-scarred valiants now traced the trip as the story was
pieced together:

Upon finding the footprints of Oncaye's brothers, they had
followed them to a place in the forest where chonta nuts had
been harvested. Bits of fur from woolly monkeys and bright-
colored feathers marked the trail where her brothers had
hunted.

Then Oncaye had discovered her mother's footprints, far
from the houses located from the air. As they followed the
footprints, Toña suddenly stopped and pointed to the ground.
"Blood!" he exclaimed. "Someone has been speared!"

Farther along they had found the fiber wrappings from
spears, a sure sign of conflict. The footprints led to a small
manioc field just off the trail, but then returned *back up the
trail.*

It had been growing late and the shadows deepened. Using
a flashlight, the party discovered "lots and lots of *men's* footprints." No further evidence was necessary; there had been
spearings in Oncaye's family group. If she went farther, she and
the others would also be speared. The four retraced their steps.
At a fork in the trail Oncaye again discovered her mother's
footprints. They indicated that she had fled up a side trail.

Leaving the men in hiding, the girls had followed the footprints to a very small house in a dense area. As they approached
it, they were stopped short by the stench of decaying flesh, and
the small clearing was filled with huge buzzards. Oncaye saw a
decaying body with spears still protruding. It must be the last
remains of her own mother. Nauseated and shocked, the two
girls turned away, weeping. Rejoining the men, they all fled for
their lives.

"Why didn't you go into the house to be sure it was your
mother?" Rachel asked naïvely after she heard the story.

"You don't know what buzzards are like! If you disturb them

in their dirty work they will bite you like mad dogs!" was the curt answer.

Besides, Oncaye had been sure; she had seen her mother's footprints, and her mother's clay cooking pot, right by the house. Of course her mother was one of those who had been speared! Tidonca had threatened long ago!

Details of the return trip to Tiwaeno were gradually told:

In need of rest, the four had stopped in the night and made a quick shelter. As they settled down, they heard noises close by. They were being followed!

The girls, who began to whisper, had then agreed on a conversation for the benefit of the unseen listeners. It went something like this:

*Oncaye:* "How sad I am! We went all that long distance to find my mother and my brothers and bring them to live happily with us and learn about God. And what did they do? They got hateful and killed them, just before we got there!"

*Boika:* "Yes, I am sad, too. If I had only listened to God when He told me to go, instead of planting my peanuts first, we might have reached them in time. I wish they would come upriver, so that we could meet them, and teach them about God . . ."

The girls had then heard a whistle in the forest: the Auca signal for attack. Silently they awakened their sleeping companions, grabbed the radio and other belongings, and started racing again toward Tiwaeno. Before she left, Oncaye, convinced that those in pursuit were her own half-brothers, had called boldly into the night,

"So you plan to spear me, too! Well, go ahead and try it! You can't hurt me. You will just kill my body and it will rot, but my soul will go to heaven to be with God!"

At a good distance away they had set up the radio and talked with Rachel.

Finally, they had been met by the Tiwaeno Christians at Fish River, and the two groups hurried upriver to Palm Beach where the downriver trail crossed the Curaray.

In 1956 five missionaries, who were attempting to reach the untamed Auca Indians, were killed by them on "Palm Beach" in the jungle of Ecuador. The murderers have given up spearings ever since they heard the Word of God—"God's Carving." Pilot Don Smith poses with them: Left to right: Nimonga, Dyuwi, Gikita, Kimo, and Minkayi. Sixth Auca (front row) is Toña.

Memorial stamps issued ten years after tragedy. Left to right: James Elliot, Pete Fleming, Nate Saint, Ed McCully, and Roger Youderian.

Auca village of Tiwaeno in Ecuador's upriver Oriente jungle was opened to outsiders through Dayuma, an Auca woman who returned after years on the outside. *Steve Saint*

Dayuma's marriage to Komi in 1961 follows Auca tradition of being "tied together in the hammock." Komi's father, Gikita (bottom center), and Don Smith (to Gikita's left) ask God's blessing on the union.

Oncaye, recently arrived from downriver, is relaxed and happy in Tiwaeno. Older sister, Boika, is in background; Boika's daughter at left.

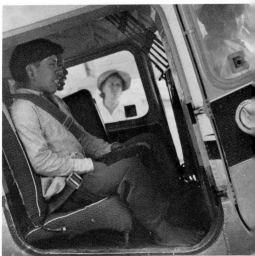

Oncaye and missionary Rachel Saint test communications gear.

Dyuwi, Kinta, and Gikita in plane, February, 1964. Rachel Saint looks on.

This thatched chapel, God's-speaking-house, was built by former Auca killers in 1964. It was later extended to accommodate the Tiwaeno population explosion as wild downriver relatives were brought in to hear God's Carving.

Dawa's drawing of her downriver relatives as seen from plane trip. Pregnant woman, who is depicted at lower left, gave birth in Tiwaeno.

Rachel translates God's Carving with Dayuma, who holds her daughter, Eva.

Dayuma's blind daughter, Eunie, sits with Dawa in Rachel's house. Dawa constantly taught her about other people, numbers, God's Carving, etc. In June, 1972, Eunie drowned in a strong current while playing in the Tiwaeno River.

Easter Sunday, 1965, is celebrated by reading the newly published Gospel of Mark. Center: Rachel Saint, Dayuma, Kimo, Phil Saint, and Don Johnson. The latter's wife, Helen, sits behind Rachel, with Dawa at her left.

Stump of tree in which slain missionaries built house in 1956. Kimo, standing at right of stump, remembers, "Here we sinned," as Steve, Phil, Oncaye, Rachel, Kathy Saint, Marj, and Kimo listen.

On jungle trail to the Curaray, where Oncaye (behind girl carrying small child) will be baptized. Also shown are Phil Saint, Rachel, and Marj Saint, widow of missionary Nate Saint.

Limoncocha Base on arrowhead-shaped jungle lake off Napo and Jivino Rivers.

Baptism at **Palm Beach**. Rachel, Steve, Marj, Phil, Kathy, and others bow their heads as Kimo (right) prays. *Gosney*

Dan Choisser, JAARS radio technician and radio operator at Limoncocha, with electronic basket improvised by him for ground contact with downriver Aucas. His wife, Ruth, is shown in radio tower at Limoncocha during contact attempts.

Tidonca and his wife, with two of his children.

Tyaento, Oncaye's "bad brother" who had wanted to kill his little daughter were his baby son to die, sits on platform of God's-speaking-house. Hammocks in back are for polio victims who come to church.

George Cowan, president of Wycliffe Bible Translators, Kimo, Komi, and Rachel attend session of World Congress on Evangelism, Berlin, November, 1966.

Sightseeing in Berlin is an unforgettable experience.

Toña at age twelve, shortly after arrival at Tiwaeno. Facial expression reflects antipathy toward outsiders.

Rachel grooms Toña to **teach** reading.

Toña, his wife, Wato, and baby daughter.

Numerals and words from Mark 16:15 were printed by Toña before he left for the Ridge to contact relatives. Planes, helicopters, and other embellishments have been added by his pupils.

Toña with manpack, as he prepares to leave for his trip.

*Barbara Youderian*

A downriver house on "Baiwa's river." *Steve Saint*

Tiwaeno Christians bring entire Baiwa group up Curaray. Here they pull up at a beach. *Sam Padilla* (***Dayuma's son***)

Dayuma at Palm Beach. She is calling in on the trail radio set to report that Baiwa's group will reach Tiwaeno the next afternoon. *Sam Padilla*

Catherine Peeke and JAARS pilot Jim Rainsberger with food supplies to be dropped to Kimo and Dawa on Baiwa trail.

Runaways from Baiwa's group returning to Tiwaeno to avoid encounter with oil explorers.

Polio epidemic struck Tiwaeno in 1969. A patient, Downriver Enae, is comforted by Dawa in Vozandes Hospital, Shell Mera. Lois Pederson, Wycliffe nurse, reports by radio to Rachel Saint in Tiwaeno.

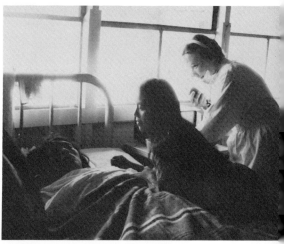

Dr. Peter Ray and volunteer nurses administer oxygen and iron-lung therapy to Enae.
*Vozandes*

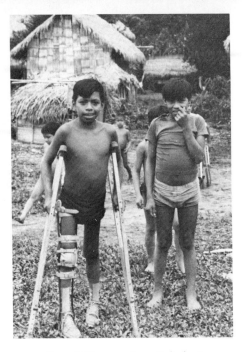

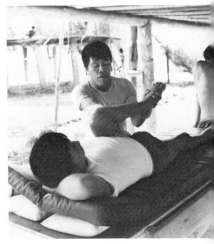

Son of Piyamo, the witch-doctor, on crutches and braces, which he later abandoned after successful therapy program at Limoncocha & Tiwaeno.

Dyuwi continues to give therapy to polio patients in Tiwaeno.

Oil camp and drilling rig in Ecuador's Oriente.

Oncaye, holding her infant, and her brother, Tewae, show strain as they are about to embark in oil company helicopter on dangerous contact to **bring Wepe and Toña from Ridge.**

Ridge Aucas on **Gaba** River airstrip.

Pilot Roy Gleason and Catherine Peeke with Wepe and Kiwa.
**The latter was impersonating Toña, who had disappeared.**

Wepe (second from right) talks to Dayuma, while Kiwa, the impostor, hangs his head after being reprimanded. Bandage on Kiwa's leg supposedly "covers" spot where Toña had received alligator bites.

A mood of anticipation fills former killer, Gikita, who has received word that his Ridge brother, the powerful witchdoctor Awaemae, soon will be joining him and the other Auca Christians in Tiwaeno. Balsa plugs once filled empty holes in earlobes.

There had been no rain for thirteen unusual days and the river was low. Dashing down the beach to a small stream, they entered their waiting canoes and poled for their lives toward a bend in the river. But their tracks were on the beach. With the enemy hot on their heels, Oncaye prayed, "God make it rain, quick!" Within a few minutes water poured from the sky. Now their footprints would disappear! The party continued to pole rapidly through the storm and arrived the same day at the crossover. Then, hurrying over the Tiwaeno trail, they reached home safely.

Exhausted but thankful for deliverance, they anticipated the next threat by the downriver Aucas.

For pilot Don Smith these events dramatized the need for air-to-ground contact. He recommended that a loudspeaker he had prepared be mounted on the wing of the plane. Rachel agreed.

By the time of the next overflight, the downriver group had burned their houses and fled to another location. A house with thirty people around it was spotted in a new clearing. As the plane circled, Oncaye called from the speaker to her people, "I am Oncaye! Being alive, I live! I am alive!" When the men on the ground responded with jabbing motions, she commanded them, "Put down your spears!" They did so, and made gestures for her to come down. She replied that she could not.

"Meet me upstream at Moipa's manioc field in peace!" Oncaye called.

The first use of the loudspeaker had been a gratifying success.

# 7 ❦ LOST DOWNRIVER

While invitations were being called to hostile downriver Aucas from the air, a request from afar reached Rachel in Tiwaeno. Christian leaders were to gather in Germany at the World Congress on Evangelism in November, 1966. Would the Auca pastor, Kimo, represent the newest church in Christendom?

At first the Aucas were apprehensive about a trip to the foreigners' land. But Kimo finally agreed to go, accompanied by Dayuma's husband, Komi, and by Rachel as interpreter.

The two men, bundled beyond recognition as jungle Indians, except for the prominent holes in Kimo's ears, and their friend, Rachel, left the warmth of Ecuador for a chilly stopover in the United States en route to a wintry Europe. At Rachel's home near Philadelphia they met Mrs. Katharine Saint, the eighty-four-year-old mother of Rachel and Nate. The Auca men had never seen such an *old* person, nor had they ever sensed more genuine human affection.

❦ Ever since the five missionaries were martyred by Aucas, Christians around the world had prayed for the savage tribe. A decade later the two Auca representatives, standing poised and fearless before twelve hundred delegates at the Berlin Congress, told with simple force of the impact of the gospel on their tribe. George Cowan, president of the Wycliffe Bible Translators, interviewed them, with Rachel interpreting.

Kimo told the Congress that his forefathers "just spoke a little about God, then they 'went off the trail.' " They had lived in fear, killing their own relatives as well as outsiders.

"Dayuma taught us God's Carving," he said. "She taught us that we should live with one wife, not with many, as our ancestors did. Now happily I live with my wife, Dawa."

Kimo emphasized his call to his savage kinsmen, and was assured of the prayer of many more friends.

Cowan wrote of the impact on the Congress: "The Aucas were terrific with their three-note melody and their simple repetitive songs. During the closing hymn an African delegate could contain himself no longer. He jumped up onto the platform and hugged each of the Auca men. I overheard one delegate say that the African had only done what everyone present wanted to do."

After the Congress the Aucas visited Wycliffe's headquarters in Germany, Switzerland, and England, where they were welcomed enthusiastically by friends who long had followed the Auca story. They finally returned to Ecuador with Rachel, eager to resume attempts at downriver contact.

The memorable journey had prepared Kimo to help Rachel and Dayuma in the translation of the Book of Acts. As they looked for words to express the phrase "unto the uttermost parts of the earth," in Acts 1:8, Kimo made valuable suggestions. Laughing, he said that when he was young all the Aucas believed that the world ended just beyond the Napo River on one side, and beyond the Curaray on the other. One of the ancestors had dared to cross the Curaray; he went a short distance and came to a place where the earth and sky met. He even reached up and touched the sky! No one doubted his word, least of all Kimo, who had heard the story directly from his grandfathers.

In December the translation of Acts was interrupted by bad news from the Napo where a Quichua had been speared by Aucas. Oncaye felt an urgency to reach the killers with God's message "before they kill again." That would change them.

In January, 1967, four Aucas led by Oncaye began another trip to the downriver houses. Dyuwi was ill, and Toña, the best reader in Tiwaeno, was teaching the others; he could not be spared. Oncaye and Dawa would attempt the contact. Kimo accompanied by Minkayi would wait at the halfway point. The party carried gifts for the relatives, who had shown signs of friendliness to those who called from the plane.

Confident of the trail, the party reached Oncaye's family area without delay. The men waited at "Kimo's beach" and the two girls took the long trail downstream to the houses. To their disappointment they found the shelters deserted, some of them in charred ruins. Fear at having been discovered caused the family to flee to another location. The girls left gifts of bright-colored cloth. Then, returning sadly to the waiting men, the four took the trail back to Tiwaeno.

Undaunted, the "believing family" continued to pray and plan. News of the spearings on the Napo went on. A further stimulus for action was the expected arrival downriver of petroleum companies long at work on the Colombian border. Since the Aucas are monolingual, communication between workers and Indians would be impossible. Unless the killers could be reached first, more spearings would ensue.

After four disappointing trips to Oncaye's home area by the Auca Christians, it became more evident that further electronic communication might be the key to a successful contact.

In October, following an overflight to an area where new downriver houses were located, another party of four prepared for a trip to the rebellious relatives.

"This time we won't get lost!" Oncaye had exclaimed at seeing the houses clearly from the plane window. She knew the river well, and the houses were *right on the river.*

Kimo and Dawa, Oncaye and Dyuwi, started out with their two-way radio. Kimo and Dyuwi hewed out a canoe at the headwaters of the river to pole their way to the houses. Several days later they radioed for a food drop. Don Smith, with Rachel and Toña, flew toward the river where the land party was supposed to be traveling. But as Don attempted to find them, the radio signal grew weaker. Finally, the party was discovered on *another* river, and the food drop was made in a deep canyon.

A high ridge separated the group from the river upon which they should have been traveling. They were off course, moving away from their goal. Guided by radio, the group finally completed their mission and returned to Tiwaeno, where they related details of the trip:

There had been a confusion in the Auca names for the two rivers, hence the mistake. Dawa and Oncaye, in their attempt to locate the place where they had previously left gifts, crossed the high ridge between the two rivers and followed the downriver trail toward the houses. The men returned by canoe to wait at the headwaters. Meanwhile, the two girls found that their earlier gifts had been taken, and recent Auca warnings left in their place! Hurrying back toward Kimo and Dyuwi by a different trail, Oncaye and Dawa saw footprints and signs which told them that a large party of downriver Auca men had come out to meet them—with spears! But the footprints turned back at the headwaters. Surely they had heard Kimo's and Dyuwi's chopping and fled, thinking the foreigners had come. If the missionary party had not been on the wrong river, they most surely would have been killed!

Rachel wondered how soon another downriver trip would be planned. The last one had been dangerous. But within a short time Dyuwi shared with the group what the Lord had told him: they were to continue until *all the Auca groups* had been reached. Then they were to go far beyond, to people who made idols with their own hands and called them gods. There the Aucas would tell them of the true and living God. That's what God wanted them to do, to carry His message to *all lands!*

# 8 ✻ "BRING ME A FOREIGNERS' AX"

Kimo, sensing the discouragement of the Tiwaeno group caused by delays in the downriver contact, talked one Sunday to his people about fishing:

"Fishing—what is it like? If you throw in your hook and leave it, you will never get a bite. If you get a nibble and the fish gets away with your bait, you put on another, or straighten the hook, change the bait, and try again. That's what it's like."

In the Auca translation the verse "Follow me and I will make you fishers of men" read: "Follow me and I will make you *gatherers* of men." The main verb in the verse meant "to gather together for a specific purpose by *calling.*" Rachel commented after Kimo's talk, "This is exactly what we had been doing from the air to the ground for months!"

Kimo urged his group to pray to God and try again.

On one of the overflights several new clearings had been spotted some distance from where Oncaye's family had first been located. One house had been built on a small hill. The pilot flew low and circled below the hilltop to aid Oncaye in identifying people on the ground. At one point he made a pass very close to the houses, the plane almost on a level with the clearing.

A young boy on the clearing spied Oncaye in the plane. He began to laugh, and galloped and jumped, galloped and jumped, in an effort to keep up with the plane.

"It's Awa, my little brother Awa!" Oncaye shouted, and she almost wept for joy. She saw some of the other younger members of the family, too, and someone who looked like her mother. But she was sure her mother had been speared!

"It must be my mother's sister," she decided.

Oncaye's earlier account of the buzzards had led Rachel to pray desperately for two-way communication with the savage Aucas. This need challenged Don Smith to contrive a transmitter to be lowered from the plane in the bucket-drop designed by Nate Saint and used by him and his four companions in early aerial contacts with the Aucas. The necessary equipment proved too heavy for this technique and was then replaced by a transmitter to be parachuted to the ground. It was encased in a container made of things at hand, a lard can, a tuna fish can, and a flashlight. An antenna arranged around a plastic salad bowl was the final component of the transmitter.

The first attempt was thrilling. Auca voices from below were clearly transmitted to the plane. But alas! The contraption landed in a tree; the Aucas retrieved it quickly and evidently ripped off the antenna, leaving only a disappointing silence.

After the disheartening loss of several such transmitters, a meeting of those involved in Operation Contact was held at Limoncocha. The issue: What could be done to overcome the Auca custom of bashing in anything *foreign?* Don Johnson's suggestion: Hide it in an Indian basket. The antenna could be woven into the basket, a false bottom constructed to camouflage the transmitter, and gifts placed on top. This would distract the Aucas as their voices were being transmitted to the plane circling overhead.

The ground-to-air device was perfected by Don Smith with technical help and equipment provided by Marion Kreckler of World Radio Missionary Fellowship at HCJB in Quito. Don later described the electronic breakthrough:

"When we put the transmitter in the basket, we hid a loop antenna in the weave of the basket. The diameter of the basket was much larger than the salad bowl. We found that this antenna was more efficient in radiation than the salad bowl antenna had been. We further found that a directional quality of the field of emisson was apparent since the strongest signal was available within a cone above the basket as it sat on the ground. The airplane as it flew overhead was circling within the envelope of strongest field strength from the basket's emission. It was an unsophisticated arrangement, but it worked beautifully."

By February, 1968, the "electronic basket" was ready for use. Landing on target in the middle of the downriver clearing, the package was pounced upon by Oncaye's family. A young girl severed the white nylon parachute, slipped it over her head, and danced around the clearing with the long white chute draped around her. To the spectators in the plane, she looked like a floating ghost! Meanwhile, a boy had grabbed the basket, run to the edge of the clearing, and disappeared with it. But Don knew the transmitter was working, for he picked up the signal as he flew over the area.

Oncaye called from the loudspeaker, "Taking the basket, bring it back! Bring the basket! Don't throw the basket away!" But her pleas went unheeded. The "phantom" continued to dance, and Oncaye saw her brother return emptyhanded to the clearing, the basket having been left in the forest.

She called again and again, but to no avail. Don circled overhead, then flew out of sight in the hope that the Aucas would respond. He flew over the clearing again.

Still no basket.

In defeat Oncaye handed the microphone to Rachel, who began to scold the Aucas on the ground like a commanding old "grandmother": "Bringing the basket, return, I tell you! Returning it, bring it to the clearing!"

Finally Don, who was about to "kick the rudder" and leave, decided to circle the area once more. Oncaye's young brother suddenly ran off again and brought back the basket. With a there's-your-old-basket gesture at the plane, he plunked it down in the middle of the clearing.

Oncaye grabbed the microphone and began to talk to a man standing by the basket.

"Who are you?" she asked.

"I am Dabu!" came the voice through the transmitter, clear as a bell.

"You are *not* Dabu, don't be talking wild! You are my own brother, Tyaento, I am your sister, Oncaye!" She could recognize his voice even after four years of separation.

Tyaento gazed at the plane in wonder. All at once he knew that his own sister was really in that Thing overhead. It was not her spirit after all. Oncaye was *alive.*

Oncaye continued to call, "We want to meet you in peace. Go toward Moipa's fields and we will meet you on the trail."

"Bring me a foreigner's ax and I will go," Tyaento bargained.

Oncaye assured her brother that they would return with the ax, and the plane left.

That same day Don flew directly to the clearing and circled low. An expectant Tyaento was waiting and gazing eagerly toward the plane. A package containing Don's own ax, sharpened and polished, dropped at his feet.

"Leaving tomorrow, in the early morning, we will meet you on the trail!" boomed Tyaento's voice through the transmitter.

Oncaye could hardly believe what she was hearing! She called out further instructions for her family, and the plane then headed for Tiwaeno. A ground party must be alerted to leave with Oncaye at once to meet her family at the midway point.

Early the next morning the Tiwaeno group set out, carrying a two-way radio and the necessary food and medicines. When they reached the meeting place four days later, there was no one there. They pushed on, and another day passed.

From Tiwaeno a flight was made toward the clearing downriver to see if the family actually left. Dayuma and Rachel were with Don Smith in the plane. Forced off route by a storm front, they flew around it and to their surprise arrived at a point exactly over the downriver houses. It was plain that Titada's house was empty; there was no sign of life below.

Looking down on that vast solid mass of trees, no one in the plane could discern where the trail from the clearing led upriver. But the weather forced Don to return the way he had come, parallel to the storm.

Suddenly, Dayuma pointed excitedly through the rising wisps of clouds ahead. "Smoke!" she exclaimed.

"That's not smoke. Those are rising wisps of clouds," was Don's unbelieving response.

Dayuma was adamant. That was *smoke.*

A second look convinced Don that she was right. Dayuma's whole strong hand pointed firmly ahead as Don now flew low over the forest. When they were over the spot she had spied, Dayuma took the microphone and called in a loud voice, "Is that you down there, Tyaento? If it is, make more smoke!" And billows of smoke began to roll up.

"I am Dayuma! Oncaye and the others are on their way to meet you! They are close by!" she continued. "Is it all right for them to come on?"

More and more smoke billowed up.

Don then flew off toward the Tiwaeno group. Estimating their position, he circled overhead, a signal to set up the radio.

"I saw their smoke in the forest!" Dayuma shouted joyfully over the radio. "They are just ahead of you, you should meet today!"

Cheered by the good news, the ground party hastened on. Oncaye and Dawa began to run in their eagerness, climbing swiftly over fallen logs and splashing through the small streams. Finally Dawa, weakened by recent illness, stopped to rest. Oncaye ran on ahead.

At last she saw footprints, then heard voices off in the jungle. Running to the edge of an opening in the trees, she saw Titada, who was carrying a clay pot of water.

"Mother!" she called.

At the sound of a voice, the Aucas in the clearing scattered in fear. Oncaye's mother, bewildered, looked first toward those who were fleeing, then toward the direction of the voice. *What was it, a devil?*

Again the voice called, "Mother!" Then Oncaye appeared.

It had been four years since Oncaye fled to the outside world. She had grown, and she even wore clothing, but Titada recognized her daughter.

"Oncaye! Is it you?" The voice was choked with emotion. "You were not killed by the outsiders after all!"

"Mother! Is it you? I thought you had been speared and eaten by the buzzards!"

Soon Dawa arrived, weary but overjoyed at seeing Titada.

As Dawa searched the clearing for the others, she spied a hammock slung between the trees and moving slightly.

"Who is that in the hammock?" she asked.

It was Wiña, Tyaento's young wife, swollen and suffering from a venomous snakebite. Too ill to travel, she lay in her hammock, waiting to die. This misfortune had forced the group to discontinue their trek toward the meeting point.

"We brought medicine for snakebites!" exclaimed Dawa with characteristic concern for the afflicted. "We will use it and pray to Father God to save her life!"

Crying with fright were Wiña's two small children, who listened to the moans of their helpless mother.

One by one Oncaye's family emerged from the forest.

There was Awa, who *knew* he had seen Oncaye that day the Thing flew past their house on the hill!

And there was Tyaento . . . *You rascal! Why did you call yourself "Dabu"?*

# 9 ✿ ENCOUNTER WITHOUT SPEARS

Wiña's swollen body indicated that the venom would soon reach her vital organs. Dawa, who had been trained by Rachel, began to administer the serum immediately. The first vial brought no favorable reaction. Dawa watched; soon a second, yet again a third injection was given.

Tyaento, Oncaye's brother, had consented to Dawa's treatment because he knew his wife, Wiña, otherwise would die. He was happy when at last the serum took effect; his wife revived as the swelling subsided. But it was urgent to get Wiña to Tiwaeno as soon as possible.

There was another reason for resuming the upriver trip. Some of the downriver Aucas had refused to take the trip to meet Oncaye because they feared foreigners. Titada's group, the twelve adults and children now being detained by Wiña's illness, had slipped away from their relatives on the pretext that they were going to hunt wild hogs. Those left behind would soon be in hot pursuit, once the deception was discovered.

Kimo and Dyuwi had been called from their waiting place to the gathering with the downriver relatives. Oncaye had assured them of a welcome by her older brothers, Tyaento and Tewae. Now Kimo offered to carry Wiña over the long trail.

✿ February 15, 1968—a day to remember in Auca history. More than twelve years had elapsed since Auca men in the two enemy groups last met—to spear. Now they met in peace, concerned about saving a life. Kimo shouldered Wiña in her hammock and the four men started upriver on the narrow trail shaded by towering jungle trees. Titada carried her grandchild in a bark sling, while the older child trotted behind them with Awa, Oncaye's young brother. It was he who had galloped in glee the day he saw his sister in the Thing that flew close to the new clearing on the hill. Other assorted half-brothers and sisters, who were the children of Niwa, Titada's husband, were now on their way to meet the upriver leader, Gikita.

Hungry and worn, they were urged to press on to a prearranged spot upriver where the Thing of the good foreigners would drop them food from the sky. Oncaye had radioed Tiwaeno news of the meeting, and a food flight was promised.

On the trail Oncaye learned that old Niwa had been killed near Father River a few months earlier by foreigners' gunfire. He had gone to spear outsiders, but died at their hands. With his dying breath he begged his sons *not* to spear anymore. After his death his brother and others, adhering to Auca custom, set about to kill his wives. In the spearing that followed, Dyuwi's half-sister, Boganai, was killed. It was her body that lay decaying the day they had been repulsed by the buzzards.

Titada had brought Boganai's orphaned sons, along with her own children, when she fled upriver. She was determined to find Oncaye whose voice she had heard from that Thing in the sky. To remain would only invite death.

Niwa's brother, joined by Niwa's other sons, had pursued Titada after she fled. Racing through the forest, they encountered a huge herd of wild hogs and stopped to kill them. Spears meant for Titada and her children fell in rage on the hogs. Upon reaching Titada, the hunters, their rage and weapons spent on the wild animals, simply ordered the runaways to go back home; they took one of Titada's daughters to cook for them.

Oncaye and the party recounted years of bloody family history as they trudged on.

Gikita, after hearing the news by radio, left for the trail with Komi to take provisions to Oncaye's people. He would soon be facing men who were determined to kill him. Eager now to tell them of God, he moved quickly with his load.

The travelers from downriver, exhausted but elated, finally reached the appointed beach and made camp. Soon Gikita and Komi arrived with more serum for Wiña, whose condition was still serious. Komi set his gun down on the beach and removed the big foreigners' boots from his weary feet. Gikita, clad only in shorts, sat on a log to look over the newcomers.

In the group from downriver was a young boy with long flowing black hair who had not been with Oncaye's family when she fled. She learned that he was a Quichua lad captured by her brothers on Father River when they had killed his father more than a year ago. Since no Auca could speak Quichua, he had learned Auca, which he now spoke fluently.

When the boy saw Komi, who was dressed like an outsider and without holes in his earlobes, he took him for a Quichua. He began pouring out his story to Komi, forgetting that he was speaking *Auca*. Komi listened sympathetically as the boy pleaded to be returned to his family. He hated the Aucas. He would kill them if he got a chance! Komi calmed the boy, saying that "we will talk to God about it." Sensing the lad's embarrassment at looking like an Auca, Komi gave him a pair of shorts and cut his long hair then and there!

Soon the promised plane appeared and a welcome food drop parachuted to the beach, right on schedule and right on target. Titada and her brood ate well for the first time in many days. The hungry Aucas devoured the food after Oncaye assured them it would not make them sick.

Oncaye's brothers gradually dropped their guard and began to relax as the men from the two enemy groups sat on logs, eating and talking. After a little sleep they would push on toward Tiwaeno; it would not be safe to tarry halfway.

Before the large group left for the last hard stretch, Kimo talked to them about God. He wanted the downriver relatives to hear about God's Carving, that wonderful Word that had changed him and Gikita and the other Aucas of Tiwaeno.

"Happily, believing God's Carving, we live. We do not kill outsiders or Aucas," Kimo told them, and they listened in wonder. "We do not live in adultery . . . we do not bury babies alive . . ."

On the trail they would hear more about the changes that had come to the relatives upriver. But now they must hurry toward the Curaray and safety. Wiña was carried in her hammock slung between the two men, Gikita and Kimo. Komi with his gun brought down jungle game for food along the way.

The travelers hurried toward Palm Beach where Dayuma would meet them with more provisions. Meanwhile, radio contact was lost between Oncaye's group and Tiwaeno. Momentous events were transpiring, and Rachel noted in her diary that three of the men who had killed her brother on Palm Beach were now on their way back home, bringing downriver killers with them. She grew concerned about the group.

Late in the afternoon of the seventh day after Oncaye had met her mother, the combined groups at last filed into Tiwaeno. All the Aucas gathered to see Oncaye's long-lost relatives. She joyfully led her family to the thatched hut next door to Rachel's house. How good it would be to live once again with her mother and her own brothers and sisters, and to teach them God's Carving! Father God had blessed their mission. Someday He would help them bring Niwa's other wives and children.

In the excitement Oncaye had neglected to inform her family of the *foreigner* living right in their midst. The unexpected sight of blue eyes and pale skin as Rachel appeared to greet the snakebitten Wiña was almost too great a shock for the weak woman. But her fears were allayed when the foreigner spoke to her in *Auca*.

Oncaye shared manioc and bananas with her family as she

instructed them in the new way of life in Tiwaeno. "God's Carving tells us. . . . We don't sing to the devils, we sing to God . . ." she told them, for her brothers chanted furiously in the night in fear of devils that flew about in the form of birds.

On their first Sunday in Tiwaeno, Oncaye brought all of her family to hear God's Carving in God's-speaking-house. There they listened to new songs, and to a new message about living without spearing. Kimo's messages included information that was new to them: "Foreigners are *real people*. They plant manioc, build houses, and drink banana drink just the way we do." Kimo was aware that the new arrivals thought, as once he had, that outsiders were extraordinary beings capable of supernatural acts. An Auca legend told of how these furry beings came up from the river, shed their fur, and turned into people who could not be killed by Auca spears. They caught Aucas in the cracks of mammoth jungle trees where they were left to die. The story ended, "Long, long ago these powerful beings became the *cowode*—outsiders!"

Oncaye's unmarried brother, Tewae, received Kimo's message and began to believe. Within a short time he married a daughter of Upriver Dabu, who continued to instruct his new son-in-law in the way of the Lord. This marriage was the first of numerous marriages between members of the two groups, including Oncaye's marriage to Upriver Dabu's son, Nangae.

Tyaento, as rebellious as Tewae was receptive, refused the new teaching. Although his snakebitten wife was recovering through constant loving care of the Tiwaeno Christians, he was hard and ungrateful. He still resented outsiders. When he therefore heard that some Quichua Indians had come to visit Aucas living on the Curaray, his old passions flared. Quichuas had killed Niwa, and he would avenge his stepfather's death. He made spears quickly in order to go at once to kill them. Ignoring the pleas of the Tiwaeno group, he thundered vile threats and insisted he would not only spear but would go back downriver forever.

He summoned his wife, Wiña, who followed him away. On-caye joined her sister-in-law, pleading silently with God to intervene. A short distance from Tiwaeno Wiña ran into a nest of large stinging ants. Their powerful, painful bites stopped her on the trail. Tyaento paused, and the two women persuaded him to turn back with them. Thus the spearing was averted.

Titada could not forget that one of her daughters was absent from the group and still living in the old way while she was enjoying Tiwaeno. Besides, she had secretly promised to return for the others if she lived well.

One June morning she decided to go downriver for her relatives. Oncaye, taking a portable two-way radio, accompanied her mother. She planned to wait at the halfway place with her foster brother, the orphan Cangowanto, who had come upriver with Titada. Saddened at the loss of his own mother, Boganai, to the buzzards, he anticipated the arrival of his older sister.

Tyaento had daringly agreed to go in the plane with Rachel to urge his half-brother to come to Tiwaeno. It was his first flight and he was terrified to look out. When the plane was over his old home clearing, he did look down, but no one was there. He guided the pilot to a place downriver twice as far from Tiwaeno. Spotting a big thatched house, Tyaento forgot his fear and called excitedly through the loudspeaker to his whole group, whom he could see gathered there for a wedding party. He asked them to meet Titada who was already coming with Oncaye toward them on the trail.

But the group failed to meet Titada on schedule. Oncaye finally radioed that some had arrived and many more were on the way. Sickness had struck, and several members of her family were burning with fever. They were traveling slowly, too ill to make shelters from the rain and also suffering from hunger.

A rescue party led by Dyuwi left Tiwaeno with provisions; they hoped to meet Oncaye's group and help ferry them by canoes up the Curaray. The first man they encountered was so sick that Dyuwi carried him on his back. The steep trail from the river was slippery, and Tiwaeno village was deep in mud. The sick were slung in hammocks under every available shelter, and blankets were hung to shield them from the chilling wind. Overnight, Tiwaeno was turned into a rescue camp, with round-the-clock nursing to save the lives of those who had barely survived the trip. They were found to be stricken with the flu, and Dawa and Rachel attended the worst cases.

There were "dozens of children, skinny and scared!" Rachel recalls of the nightmare. They were mostly orphans, their parents having been speared. The adults were thin and undernourished. Everyone was given food and clothing, and medicine as needed. The newcomers marveled at the health of the Tiwaeno dwellers.

"How are you all so fat?" they wanted to know.

"Believing in God, we live happily now," was the simple answer. "Here we do not live in adultery . . . We *do* go to God's-speaking-house on Sundays . . . Here we do not kill . . ."

Slow in returning was Cangowanto. He went right to Rachel and said solemnly, "Nimu, I want to live in your house." Sensing a problem, Rachel took him in. Later she learned that after Titada left to go upriver the first time, two of the remaining group became sick and died. The witch-doctor was blamed and they speared him and his family, a total of eight people. Cangowanto's sister and her husband were among them. The killers were from every downriver family *now in Tiwaeno,* with even the very young boys having taken part. Ten of the enemy group had escaped to the forest, a splinter group that had not joined in the exodus to Tiwaeno.

In the food crisis caused by the influx of eaters, supplies were parachuted to the Tiwaeno clearing. It was not safe for a pilot to land, for the men from downriver were still murderers at heart. Rachel was grateful for CARE food sent from the United States to supplement the local supply of manioc and monkey meat. She had never dreamed that so many downriver people would all come at once.

The violent epidemic continued for six weeks before abating. Rachel one day was able to take a census in Tiwaeno, the once peaceful village now rocked by a cultural revolution. When she had first arrived in 1958, a remnant of 56 Aucas lived on the clearing. This number had increased to 104 by 1968. Titada brought twelve on her first trip, and 92 on the next. This total of 104 from Oncaye's group had thus *doubled* the population of Tiwaeno.

But the problems also had *more* than doubled. Many of the relatives, as soon as they were able to move about, again showed their deep-rooted hostility. Reviving old family grudges, they threatened to kill Kimo and Komi and others in Tiwaeno.

There was one bright spot. After three months Tyaento had finally agreed to let Dayuma return the captured Quichua boy to his mother—in exchange for a huge aluminum cooking pot. No one knew if his mother were still alive and living in the same place, but great preparations were made for the plane trip to the Napo. New clothes were provided for the lad who had worn none for almost two years. The Tiwaeno Aucas would send gifts for his family.

Rachel was concerned about a different kind of preparation. The twelve-year-old had learned vengeance from the down-river Aucas. He was filled with hatred for those who had speared his father. Before he flew away she took him aside and told him that the Aucas had brutally speared *her* brother. "But God asks us to forgive, as He forgave us, sending His only Son to die in our place." God had even let her come to her brother's killers to help them.

As the plane landed at the far end of the field near the Quichua village on the Napo River, one of the Indians recognized the missing boy. The Quichuas crowded around and Dayuma grasped the opportunity to address them in their own language. "You see, now some of the Aucas are good. Do not talk of killing my people anymore. Some are still bad, but we are teaching them God's Carving."

Her speech was interrupted by the rising crescendo of a Quichua death wail, but this time the words were different. *My son! My son! I thought you were dead and now I see you alive again!* The boy's widowed mother was welcoming her "resurrected" son.



In Tiwaeno, Dyuwi preached strongly against the old patterns of adultery. Potential trouble brewed when one of the married newcomers wanted to take Dyuwi's young daughter as a second wife.

"You may spear me for saying this," he declared openly, "but God's Carving says we are not to live that way!"

Uncle Gikita had invited Downriver Gikita with his family to share his food, shelter, and possessions. But when the new settler already with two wives wanted to share Uncle Gikita's wife, and his sons wanted to share Uncle Gikita's married daughter, the oldest man in Tiwaeno drew the line. Leaving all of his planted fields and his home to Downriver Gikita, Uncle Gikita took his family to the Curaray and started all over again. This involved clearing a virgin forest, but Uncle Gikita had vowed long ago not to spear and to follow God's Carving wholly.

Many of the new group were closely related to Dawa. In the Auca kinship system she was "grandmother" to many, though she herself had no children and was younger than many of her relatives. This role carried authority, which Dawa used for God. "By day she exhorted and admonished them," Rachel recalls, "and by night she checked to see if they were in their hammocks and not out trying to kill someone."

In one showdown an illegitimate newborn was about to be thrown into the river. Dawa intervened courageously and restrained the murder-bound mother-in-law. The child was returned to its mother.

One day Tyaento was found sharpening his spears to kill his

little daughter if his baby son should die. The sick child was sent in the plane with his mother, Wiña, to the clinic at Limoncocha. The child lived, and another tragedy was prevented.

Kimo was shocked at this display of brutality and came to Rachel, stating, "If that's the way they are going to act, I'm *through* bringing in other Auca groups!"

Rachel reminded him of God's Carving and of Tyaento's need of a new heart.

After reflecting awhile, Kimo said, "All right. Following God, I will go again to call others, no matter what happens!"

# 10 ❧ "LIQUID FIRE" AND "BIG BIRDS"

At the height of the cultural collision between the upriver and downriver groups, Catherine Peeke, who had gone to the States to complete her Ph.D. in linguistics at Indiana University, returned to Tiwaeno. She found Rachel's time "more than monopolized by constant social, medical, and spiritual crises, and in averting conflict and arranging provision for the homeless."

Tiwaeno Christians were almost overwhelmed by their demanding deceptive relatives. "Their poultry is depleted almost to the point of no return, half-developed vegetables disappear from their gardens, and entire crops are harvested in the owner's absence," Catherine noted.

"They've eaten up every scrap of my manioc!" complained Dayuma's Aunt Maengamo. "And then you talk about calling for still more downriver relatives to come here! I should say not! There's nothing left to feed them!"

Dayuma, busy with three small daughters and a husky husband to feed, still found time to help Rachel translate the Book of Acts when the pressure lightened. Calling the signals from behind the scenes, she often kept the two groups from clashing.

Dyuwi was undaunted by the problems and complaints. Seated on the palm floor of God's-speaking-house—the building had now been extended to accommodate the untaught newcomers—he announced one Sunday in October:

"Some of you are saying, 'How could we ever meet other relatives who live still farther downriver?' I tell you, when God says it's time, trusting Him, we will meet them. *Let's trust Him!*"

Increasing overflights were being made by JAARS pilots as the location of other Auca houses was established. Tiwaeno Christians, dropping gifts from the planes, called to the Aucas not to kill the men looking for oil—"liquid fire"—and invited them to live near Tiwaeno. Dyuwi, Kimo, and Dawa were always enthusiastic and earnest in their pleas to the Aucas. But the latter often displayed hostility toward the voices of whoever-they-were whizzing low in that Thing that was looking directly down on them!

"Asking for more homeless thieves?" Catherine wrote to friends. "Dyuwi, Kimo, and Dawa, besides lacking food, also suffer pilfering, weather threat of spearing, endure malicious gossip. It was they who tramped over rugged jungle miles to search out the group who have now responded. It is they who teach untiringly, rise at midnight to administer pills or check on prowlers. And it is they who will go again the long way to meet the lost and welcome them in Jesus' name."

By December, 1968, a number of "huge houses with lots of naked Aucas" had been located on a master map of Aucaland that Rachel and Catherine were making. Although they had not yet flown over all the flat jungle and heavily wooded ridges included in Auca territory, they were sure of two more main settlements: a large group of houses in the lower Curaray area, and another cluster of dwellings on what was designated "the Ridge," both groups of Aucas right in the path of oil exploration pressing in from north and south.

The perfected electronic basket formed an indispensable link with the Indians on the ground. For Rachel it was fantastic to hear a chorus of Auca voices crowding the air waves and registering loudly in the plane. There was one recurring refrain: "Throw me down an *ax* . . . a *machete* . . . some *beads* . . . 'when they ripen on the bushes.' " Impressed by the appearance of the bright glass beads in the gift drops, the Aucas thought this new item had actually grown on bushes.

Some of the friendly voices from the ground called, "We will come, carrying just a blowgun!" Others invited the aerial visitors to come down and take them for a ride.

Of the increased number of flights over the vast area Catherine wrote: "It's a trick to keep up with the Aucas' frequent movements, but it is essential, in view of the imminent oil explorations. We try to warn the Aucas to avoid conflict when they encounter outsiders, as they are bound to do, sooner or later. Our efforts are feeble in light of historical accounts that invariably record conflict. And when you consider that the warning is shouted by a roaring, raging beast that they have long considered to be a demon, the chances of their heeding is small indeed."

Oil exploration forced an acceleration in expensive overflights. Each trip involved about five hours of flying time. "The oil companies," Catherine continued, "stand to benefit from peaceful contact and generously cooperate in making the flights. There are several productive wells north of the Napo River, so they are ready to go all out for the territory to the south. Actually, four oil companies are involved, and their interests converge *at the Auca houses.*"

In addition to planes, helicopters were used by the oil companies to penetrate the jungle. Their trails were marked by helipads every three miles. On several occasions the "big birds" aided in the rescue of isolated Aucas who were dangerously ill.

Downriver Dabu had been a rebel since his arrival in Tiwaeno with the second group of Oncaye's family. He did not like the new code of morals and rejected God's Carving. He separated himself from the Christians and went over to live on Fish River, along with his old mother and younger brother.

During that time, and after six years of delay, the land that had been requested from the government by Dayuma's group was finally designated an Auca Protectorate. It was only onetenth of the total territory held by the Aucas for many centuries. But oil exploration was now entering the Protectorate. To avoid conflict, Dayuma recalled all the downriver Aucas to the

Tiwaeno clearing. However, they brought word that Dabu the Rebel was detained on the trail. He had been bitten by a poisonous snake, and the flesh around the bite was rotting. He was also ill with flu, which was turning into pneumonia. He was unable to travel and would die without help.

A reconnaissance helicopter flight made by an oil company pilot and his assistant located Dabu in a hut down in a narrow ravine. It would be impossible to reach him except in a hovering helicopter. The pilot suggested that he drop a rope ladder by which the sick Indian could climb into the craft. But Catherine knew that Dabu would be too weak for such an effort, and besides, he had never seen a roaring demon at close range!

Oncaye and other Christians from Tiwaeno then went on foot to the tiny clearing of Dabu the Rebel. They gave him medication and food, and told him that a "big bird" would return to take him out.

Catherine described the rescue:

"The pilot kept settling in lower and lower, until he was about three or four feet from the ground. Then I was sort of handed down to the ground where I rounded up the scared Aucas who had hidden from the 'big bird' in the trees at the edges of the ravine. It's really frightening, for they don't cut the motors and you have to go under the rotor.

"The Indians rallied and fell to clearing the low jungle growth. The copter settled in and waited for us to get rounded up. With those big blades roaring around, Dabu wasn't in a frame of mind to listen to me, but his family talked him into getting aboard. The old mother got aboard without a fuss, but she was trembling. The younger brother followed, and they were all set to bring the dog—but I figured it would make it over the trail with the rest who wouldn't fit in the copter.

"The horribly little space was really quite ticklish for take-off —only about three times the length of the chopper and just barely wide enough for the rotors—and it was pouring rain. We were most thankful to get out of there.

"In no time we were in Tiwaeno, and all hands were on deck to greet us. . . . The rescue has won the Aucas' hearts for those who are operating the helicopters.

"This thing costs $200–$300 an hour to run; and it was a three-hour operation—besides the four high-priced employees! The oil people, in turn, are more than willing to do what they can for our operation, since we have almost cleared their whole concession of Aucas. They assure us that they aren't just being generous!"

Dabu the Rebel reached Tiwaeno just as another severe flu epidemic was beginning to subside. The group from downriver, exposed for the first time to outsiders' diseases, had suffered under wave after wave of illness since their move to Tiwaeno.

One woman who had been very ill began to act abnormally. The Aucas reported that she spoke of having seen a certain bird, and the demons were claiming her.

"By afternoon she was out of her head, just plain crazy!" Rachel wrote in a letter to friends. "Her family said it was the devils, and the next day I was ready to agree with them. We had to take her baby away from her and tie the woman in her hammock. We even tried a dog chain to keep her from running off and drowning herself. She became dumb and could not talk.

"During the Sunday morning service she became worse. She was in the hammock near the meeting, which was being disrupted. Dayuma was telling the story of the Gadarene, and I found myself asking the Lord to do what He had done for the demon-possessed man. I looked around—no pigs in Tiwaeno, but there was Dayuma's monkey under the thatched roof. 'Lord, send those devils into the monkey—if they have to be in some being!' The patient quieted down and the monkey began to carry on such as no monkey ever had done. He raced up to the church platform and clung to the nearest Auca, chattering wildly. Dayuma finally interrupted her story to throw the monkey off—and it began to rave at *her!* After that the afflicted woman began to improve, very slowly."

# 11 ❀ "I'LL SEPARATE THEIR SOULS FROM THEIR SKINS!"

With the arrival of the last group of Oncaye's people an information gap in Auca history was bridged.

For many years the feuding tribe had been forming into new groups. Family names, however, were retained. When the Auca Christians in Tiwaeno began to question the newcomers about family ties, Dawa learned that her brother, Baiwa, had fled from Titada's group about ten years before. He had taken relatives with him, and was probably hiding out in the forest to the south. That her family might have survived tribal spearings excited Dawa.

Titada and Rachel went on a flight in December, 1968, over houses discovered in the area where Baiwa's group had gone. The plane, almost grazing the treetops, slowed as the pilot banked steeply to give Titada a good look. Breaking out in loud, ballistic Auca, she pointed down and shouted *"Baiwa! It is Baiwa! Baiwa!"* and her voice floated from the loudspeaker to the startled Indians below.

Naked women and children bolted in fright, but Baiwa stood firm. Gazing upward, he waved and shouted at the Thing that was spying on them from the sky.

The river near which the group lived—nameless on the maps of Ecuador—was designated as "Baiwa's river," another crucial location to be marked on the master map of all the Auca groups. Simultaneously with the map being made in Tiwaeno, another one was being prepared by the oil industry, a mosaic of aerial photographs of the same area, to be used in exploration. Crews and equipment, including helicopters, were pushing into the Aucas' land. It was urgent once again to warn untamed Indians of the foreign thrust into their backyard. Numerous flights would have to be made to those in forest haunts. They must be invited to come upriver to live in peace with Dayuma's people.

Downriver Dabu was taken on one of these early flights in December to call to a group on "Baiwa's river." At the mention of "Dabu" eight husky Auca men grabbed their spears and ran to an open beach. In the bright afternoon sun they looked like bronzed warriors ready for attack. Rachel recollects the frightening pantomime:

"They galloped wildly and tossed their spears toward the plane, with hatred in every movement. I remember thinking of Palm Beach—it must have been like that. They were shouting and yelling, although we could not hear their voices in the plane. I recall thanking the Lord that we were high above them in a plane—but if the plane went down, we wouldn't stand a chance. I felt the fury of it. It looked like 'all hell broke loose'! I knew that ahead was a fight against 'principalities and powers.' I was mindful that the Tiwaeno group were *asking* for it—*they* would have to cope with it."

Rachel flew again over "Baiwa's Palm Beach" to drop an electronic basket so Kimo could talk to those on the ground. Beautiful gifts of beads, mirrors, and knives were tied to the basket in an effort to pacify the Indians.

The basket parachuted down but caught in the top of a tall tree. The transmitter was working beautifully, for Kimo could hear his own voice coming *back into the plane* through it! He kept yelling to the men to cut the basket down from the tree and take it to the beach. But they waited by the river for more gift drops.

Finally, one man climbed the tree and tried to get the basket, but complained that the "cloth [parachute] was stuck" and gave up.

Rachel took the microphone and urged the Indians to get the basket. Suddenly, a man ran into a nearby house, grabbed an old basket, came running back and plopped it down in the middle of the beach.

"Not that basket . . . get *Kimo's* basket!" Rachel called. "Taking a knife, cut the basket down from the tree!"

Another man at last climbed the tree reluctantly, cut the branches, and freed the basket. All the while he could be heard fussing about how *hard* it was stuck!

Then came the words, "Baiwa has it! Baiwa has it!" Wonderful confirmation of the exact location of Dawa's brother, Baiwa! Kimo also learned that Dayuma's sister, Omatoki, was still alive and now married to Baiwa. And some of Kimo's own nephews were on the same clearing. They had all been separated from the Tiwaeno group years before by intertribal spearing.

But another voice was heard and recorded on the tape, which was analyzed later in Tiwaeno. The deep bass voice declared, "I am as hot as fire!"—furious at this foreign intrusion! Then in heightened anger, "They are foreigners, you fools! I'll separate their souls from their skins!"

Dawa recognized her brother, Babae's, voice. She had learned that Babae, too, had fled with Baiwa, after Niwa had stolen his wife, Boganai, with their then-infant son, Cangowanto. She prayed earnestly and often with the Tiwaeno Christians that her brother would "cool off" and agree to join them.

# 12 ⚜ "TOÑA, WHO'S CALLING?"

Early in 1969, during several important flights, some of the groups on the Ridge were identified. Since air-to-ground contacts depended on the small battery-powered transmitter, it was vital that the life of the battery be extended. All subsequent transmitters were therefore equipped with VOX Control. With this device the sound of the voice activates the relay, closing the battery circuit and resulting in the operation of the transmitter.

On January 20 when Rachel and Dawa were on a flight, Rachel pushed a precious electronic basket out of the plane and pulled the parachute cord. The wind carried it away from the target clearing, beyond a manioc patch and into the jungle. It finally caught and swung high in the top of the tallest tree on a ridge near the clearing.

A gift drop was made, accompanied by many shouts to the Aucas on the ground to get the basket from the tree, but they refused to budge.

Finally, a second basket was parachuted with extra care and it floated successfully to the middle of the clearing. But the "ghostly apparitions" were too much for the superstitious Indians, who refused to go near it.

The plane circled, time ticked away, and fuel was running low.

"We have just five more minutes!" Rachel sighed in despair.

After a few more entreating shouts from the plane, two youngsters picked up the basket and carried it slowly toward a group of older folks standing beside a house on the hilltop. A few remarks were shouted back and forth, but the youngsters' words were garbled. Those in the plane flew away, discouraged.

There was one ray of hope: perhaps the tape would yield some information when the relatives at Tiwaeno listened to it. But when Rachel arrived home and played the tape, she found that the recorder had not worked well.

During the night as she reflected upon the frustrating results of the flight, she listened again to the tape. Through the static came the words, *Toña, who's calling?* Rachel could scarcely wait until morning.

Yes, confirmed the Aucas, that's what the voice had said, *Toña* . . . an Auca name, and also the name of one of their own, right here in Tiwaeno. Whose son might the other Toña be, over there on the Ridge? One thing was sure: both of the *Toñas* must be named for the same grandfather! The name *Toña* would be important on future contacts with the Ridge Aucas. "We praise the Lord for this token!" Catherine exclaimed.

On her next flight Dawa assured the people that another Toña and his mother, Miñi, were "living with us, they are living well." When the name Toña was heard on the ground, an old man and woman hung their heads and appeared to be weeping.

"I wish *our* Toña could have been in the plane with us to call to them," Dawa said upon her return to Tiwaeno.

But Toña and his wife, Wato, were far down the Tiwaeno River, planting peanuts. On January 30, however, pilot Bruce Linton flew Toña, Miñi, and Catherine to the location. Miñi wore big white balsa earplugs for the occasion. Calling to her people, she announced that she and her son, Toña, had come to "visit." The Aucas, upon seeing her earplugs, listened with unusual attention.

Toña took the microphone and spoke commandingly:

"I, Toña, come. I, the one who was born the son of Miñi, I come. I, born the son of Coba, I come. Motion to me, in recognition!"

Many arms shot up and the Aucas waved vigorously, eyes fastened on the plane.

Then, singling out a man in the crowd, whom he assumed to be his older brother, Wepe, Toña called:

"Wepe, if it is you, wave to me. Don't spear the outsiders. Let them alone. Don't go out to them. I came to see you, later I will come to get you. Wave to me. Yes, to you I say, I was born your brother. Don't go to the outsiders' houses, just stay at home. I am Toña!"

After holding a tight circle as Toña talked, the plane flew away for a brief "cooling off" period during which Catherine asked him if he wanted to speak again. *"Again!"* was the emphatic reply. Thus Toña resumed:

"I left here long ago. I saw you long ago when I was a child. After being grown, I believed in God; and now I am coming to you. What about Caiga? If he's still living, motion to me."

"They're *motioning!*" Miñi exclaimed as the people pointed to one in the crowd.

"Yes," Toña continued, "since Caiga is still alive, I shall come and visit. When you see me standing at your house, come emptyhanded, without spears. Throwing away your spears, come. Upriver, where Moipa used to live, come there. If you'll come, swing your hammocks there, and I'll come to your home . . . let me come."

Then Toña asked again about his uncle, Caiga:

"Caiga, if it is you, wave, I tell you! Caiga! Come outside and let me see you! Caiga, I want to see you!"

Miñi, who continued to peer down at the gathering, now said, "Oh! He's coming!" and cupping her hand like a microphone, she yelled, "Caiga! Caiga! Caiga!" Toña also called over the loudspeaker, "Caiga, do you hear? I am the one who was Coba's son! I've come well to visit you!"

A strong-looking older man strode down a path to the middle of the clearing and waved energetically. This must be Caiga, and Toña prepared to talk to him. But the fuel was low and the plane had to go. Great excitement followed in Tiwaeno as Toña and Miñi recounted the heartening discovery of their family on the Ridge. And as the Auca kinship pattern was pieced together, Wepe turned out to be Oncaye's real *father*. It had been her *foster* father who was killed downriver.

On January 31 Kimo flew with Dawa over a clearing near Wepe's. They dropped a basket transmitter, which landed well and immediately began relaying information to the plane. People asked over and over about Titada, and one man identified himself as the son of Titada. So Oncaye's brother lived down there! As Dawa called, identifying herself, she found that her sister, Cawo, was also there.

Several more transmitters were "planted" in February and March. At one clearing communication between Toña and Aucas on the ground was especially excellent. A husky Auca named Gaewa had suddenly discovered that the basket was linked with voices coming from the plane. He built a crude platform on which that particular basket was carefully placed each time the plane returned. It was high enough to discourage the curious from tampering with it, and was the first transmitter to be left intact. It served for ten weeks.

Another trip to Gaewa's location was described in a letter by Catherine: "Weather was extremely bad, so that we were over clouds most of the way, with breaks only at crucial points like the Cononaco River, so we could drop down and follow toward the north Ridge. The Ridge itself was closed in. In fact, so many of the ridges were capped by low clouds that we finally gave up and started to leave."

But Catherine then recognized the outline of the land; they were over the clearing for which they had been searching. "There it was, just as if the Lord had brought us right out of the confusion of the hills into the valley where the houses stood!"

She also found that the transmitter parachuted to the Aucas many days before was still working.

Toña called from the loudspeaker, introducing himself and asking for identification of those on the clearing. As each name was given he answered, "All right, I understand. I am Toña . . ."

Catherine recollected, "It had been worth it to struggle through the clouds to find the place, and as I saw Toña begin to operate, I could see that it was more than worth it." She characterized his handling of the equipment and contact with his people as "a very impressive performance." The information gained was even more impressive: people all along the north Ridge turned out to be closely related to Oncaye's group, as well as to the other Tiwaeno folk.

During the contact Gaewa, son of Caiga, mentioned that he was going to visit Nampawae, and he pointed off in another direction. Nampawae—the name of Toña's brother-in-law!

Could it be that Nampawae's wife, Omade, Toña's older sister, still lived, somewhere on that rugged Ridge?

# 13 ❧ "WE *AUCAS* HAVE COME ALONE"

By the spring of 1969 oil trails had chewed through the jungle to within twenty-five miles of Baiwa's large clearing. The overland trail to Baiwa's would soon be severed. There was sure to be trouble if the Indians were not moved.

When finally a six-week deadline was given by oil company officials, Kimo and Dawa knew that they must try to persuade Baiwa and his people to come upriver. By this time aerial communication with two large groups had been established, and a land trip to reach one of them was necessary.

Kimo and Dawa had each separately made the decision to go, fully aware of the danger involved. Dawa, despite frail health, put self-consideration aside. Oncaye's sister, Ongimae, volunteered to accompany them to help carry Dawa's load on the last stretch of the trip. Kimo, who had helped spear Baiwa's parents, would let his wife make face-to-face contact with her brothers.

On July 7, 1969, Kimo and Dawa piled a limited supply of food and the indispensable two-way radio into their small canoe. With young Ongimae, they began to pole the long way down the Tiwaeno stream toward the confluence with the Curaray.

Back in the United States on the same day, astronaut Neil A. Armstrong and his teammates at Cape Kennedy were entering a modern-age craft that would land on the *moon*. *Both* trips were loaded with carefully calculated risks!

Reaching the Curaray, Kimo's party left the canoe and crossed over by trail to the headwaters of "Baiwa's river," where Kimo chopped out a second canoe for traveling down the winding river to Baiwa's location. It was a five-day undertaking, and before they left the tiny slit made in the jungle by the felling of the mighty canoe tree, a radioed request for food was met.

As they traveled they began to relate the contour of the land with that seen from the plane: they were now in Baiwa's area. But there were no signs of life, no habitations.

Finally spotting a thatched roof, they poled rapidly down the river to the small clearing and found an Auca house, *empty:* it had not been used in a long time. They had been hoping for someone from Baiwa's group to meet them as agreed during the last plane trip. Instead, they were greeted by an empty house.

The three discouraged Aucas disembarked and sank onto the sandy bank. They discussed the sad prospect of turning back with no contact. The group had evidently decided to run to some other hideout. In fact, it might be dangerous for anyone here.

Dawa started to rise wearily. She suggested that they should leave *now.* As she looked across the river, something caught her eye. No, it couldn't be, or *was* it a *poganta,* a palm-fiber headband left by her family? Hurrying through the water, she picked the headband from the tree where it had been placed, her hands trembling with excitement. Yes! *It was a poganta,* made by her very own family and left there for *her.* It had been put there about four days before; she could tell—it had dried out just about that long.

Revived by this tangible token of contact with her brothers, Dawa abruptly left Kimo sitting on the beach with the radio and started to run with Ongimae down a trail leading away from the beach. Surely there would be other signs; they must be getting near Baiwa's clearing. At a fork in the barely discernible trail she found *another poganta.* Now they must be almost there . . . which way would the clearing be? Climbing up the hill through the thickness, Dawa spied an opening among the trees. Yes, that must be Baiwa's!

She approached the clearing, and upon hearing voices, gave the Auca call *"Uuuooo"* to announce her presence. An Auca man came out of the nearest thatched house to see who had arrived.

It was her brother, Babae. Dawa knew him immediately, but he failed to recognize her. It had been almost twenty years since they had seen each other; besides, Dawa wore clothes.

"Who are you?" Babae asked in his deep bass voice.

"You guess!" was the impish answer.

"Who is that with you?"

"Ongimae."

"Who is *she?*"

"She is Titada's daughter. I went and got her."

Babae was puzzled and kept asking Dawa who she was. She in turn kept teasing her brother with *Guess! You guess!*

Finally, an old grandmother who overheard the conversation came out of the house and recognized Dawa. Turning to Babae, she scolded, "You don't even recognize *your own little sister!*"

Babae laughed and said that she looked like a foreigner. "And I suppose you have brought foreigners with you right here to our place," he added.

It was plain that he still hated foreigners—he still wanted to "separate their souls from their skins."

"Do you think I want to leave my corpse on your clearing?" his sister challenged. "We *Aucas* have come alone."

Dawa and Ongimae were finally invited into Babae's house. It was late evening, and they were offered food and drink. The girls would also spend the night. But had they really come *alone?* Dawa told Babae that Kimo was at the beach where they had found the *poganta* and was waiting for them at the empty house.

"Why have you come?" Babae asked.

"To tell you about God's Carving," was the reply.

"Who told you?"

"Dayuma."

"Dayuma—we thought she died long ago!"

"No, Dayuma is alive!"

"Who told Dayuma?"

"Nimu did."

"Who is Nimu?"

"Nimu is from the outside. She is a foreigner."

"Where is she now?"

"She lives in Tiwaeno with us."

The listening group burst into uproarious laughter.

"What? You have an outsider *living* in Tiwaeno with you?"

"Yes," Dawa explained, "this is the foreigner who came with Dayuma. They have taught us about God, we live happily now, believing."

Back at the beach, Kimo became anxious when Dawa failed to return at sunset, and he radioed Tiwaeno. He told Rachel of his fear that Dawa had been killed by Baiwa's group and of his desire to search for her body. But Rachel, hoping for further word, persuaded him to wait there until morning.

All night long, as Dawa and her skeptical family group lay in their hammocks under the big thatched roof, she talked of happy childhood days. "Remember the time we went with Father over to Fish River and Baiwa killed that big boa?" she said. The sad events that had separated them were also recalled.

Their fears faded as they reminisced and laughed. But Dawa was here on a mission. She began gently to persuade them to go with her to Tiwaeno. She told them of the foreigners who were coming to put down big pipes to suck the "liquid fire" out of the earth. It would be safer for them to be with the other Aucas now living well. "And, Babae! Your *son* is in Tiwaeno!"

As early dawn began to light the dark forest, Dawa's family talked about leaving right away for upriver. Even Babae was willing to take his chances with his sister's group, especially since the Aucas could not *talk* with outsiders. At least the foreigner living in Dawa's group could speak Auca!

Dawa had repeatedly inquired about Baiwa. Where was he?

But her people would not tell her. Now Dawa needed to know. Her husband was out there on a lonely beach, waiting by himself. Dawa would not go to report to Kimo until she knew how *all* of her family felt about the move. In fact, she was determined to wait until *all* of them would go with her.

Finally, Babae told Dawa that Baiwa was off fishing on another river with his family. He said reluctantly that they would call him. Dawa then went happily to report to Kimo.

The sight of Dawa "resurrected" and coming toward him on the beach revived Kimo. News that the *whole* group would be going to Tiwaeno was radioed to the "believing family" who were praying constantly for a peaceful contact. Arrangements were made for food drops for the large number of travelers—fifty or more! Dawa was not sure how many there were in Baiwa's large group.

Eventually Baiwa was located with his wife and children, and they joined Kimo and Dawa. Kogi, another of Dawa's brothers, showed up with his two wives and their children, some of them very young. Other relatives from houses in Baiwa's area were rounded up. They stuffed their few belongings into woven fishnets for the move to "enemy" territory. Mothers carried their babies in bark slings, and toddlers trotted beside them on the trail.

The meeting with Kimo and Dawa who were waiting on the beach to receive them was subdued and peaceful. It was on this beach only a few months before that Rachel had seen from the plane the frightening pantomine of spears. The change was indeed dramatic.

As they prepared for the long trip upstream on July 30, a supply of medicine and machetes was parachuted to them. Catherine and Titada had been on a flight to the Ridge, where they located two more groups of houses and gathered clues of identity important to Toña's family. The pilot had then located Baiwa's group on the river beach and dropped the supplies requested by Kimo in a radio contact the day before. An excited Titada yelled lustily down at her daughter, Ongimae.

The tiniest children were soon loaded into the canoe and the Auca move began. Later, when poling against the current proved too slow, the entire group took to the dense trail. The Indians hacked their way slowly westward. Kimo and Dawa prayed constantly that no one would be bitten by snakes, a bold request in so infested a place.

The food supply was soon depleted. Arriving at a clearly definable spot in the route upriver, Kimo radioed for a further food drop. The plane came, but the food landed in the river and was lost. Another drop was made farther upstream, but the parachute failed to open and the food was smashed to bits upon impact. Only a few scraps of banana were recovered and given to the youngest children, who were crying with hunger.

Many days had passed since Baiwa and his group left their downriver dwellings. They were still far from their goal and were growing weaker from lack of nourishment. If help did not come soon, there would be bloodshed in the camp. The Christians in Tiwaeno again were alerted, and promised to meet the group on the Curaray with food. Would it be possible for them to hold out a few more days?

In Tiwaeno a miniature Bible conference had been in progress with Ben Saint, Rachel's pastor brother from the States. He baptized Toña's mother, Miñi, who some months before had asked the Lord to wash her heart clean. Dayuma's Aunt Mintaka, the older woman who had been with Nate Saint and his friends on Palm Beach, was also baptized, a rewarding occasion for Nate's brother, Ben!

With word of the emergency in the returning group interrupting the happy conference, the course of events was abruptly changed. Komi announced, "I am going to leave *today* to go and meet them!" The conference was summarily abandoned as Komi and Dayuma left for the Curaray, where they loaded four canoes with provisions. Dayuma's son, Sam, now living with his mother in Tiwaeno, was eager to assist in the rescue of the downriver relatives. He went along to help pole a canoe. Other Christians also joined the river rescue party. They hurried down the Curaray with the current toward the group.

Kimo and Dawa continued to encourage their relatives up the difficult trail. The time came one night for the birth of a baby, child of Dawa's brother, Kogi. Hearing that the young mother planned to throw the child in the river—travel was already *too hard*—Dawa intervened. She pleaded with the mother, and finally declared she herself would carry the baby girl to Tiwaeno. The child was snatched from death, and the journey resumed.

Kimo and Dawa struggled to keep Baiwa and Babae under control until the Auca Christians could bring help. Remembering Babae's hot, angry words picked up by the electronic basket, Kimo knew that this untamed Auca's temper could ignite again. Nine days of hunger and fatigue since Baiwa's group had headed upstream left the men completely demoralized.

Dayuma and the others from Tiwaeno finally reached the rendezvous spot and began unloading the canoes. They hoped Kimo's group would soon arrive, and also that Baiwa's group had not turned on Kimo.

As Dayuma lifted a big cooking pot out of the canoe, she heard a noise in the forest. *"Uuuooo!"* It was Dawa! She broke through the forest and walked toward Dayuma. Then Kimo appeared, followed by fifty-six Aucas of all ages, alive but hungry.

Dayuma's canoes had arrived twenty minutes before Baiwa's group reached the meeting place!

Kimo stepped onto the beach and sank down wearily. The date was August 8, 1969. Astronaut Armstrong had beaten him. His "one small step for a man" had dropped Armstrong to the surface of the moon on July 21, 1969. But Kimo's step onto the Curaray beach symbolized "one giant leap" in Auca history!

The final lap of the trip was a saga in itself. Poling up the Curaray were a total of almost sixty people in nine canoes. Dayuma's son, Sam, described his participation: "In my canoe were Babae's whole family, plus my mother, and baby sister, with Komi poling up front and me at the back. Babae is Dawa's brother and she hadn't seen him for many years. And I didn't think I would ever see him! We got to be good friends. He used to be very mad when the plane dropped the electronic basket. We thought he was going to be the same way on the trip, but his whole attitude changed."

To supplement the short food supply on the slow journey, Komi and Sam shot wild turkeys for the hungry downriver Aucas who disdained the foreigners' repulsive food. Driven by hunger to eat it, they smelled it first and demanded, "What's this? What will happen to me if I eat *this?*" Adults often refused it, but hungry children ate the outsiders' strange stuff.

When at last they reached Palm Beach, Dayuma dug manioc from her fields planted around a bend in the river. Greatly cheered and nourished by a generous supply of this welcome jungle "manna," the Auca multitude continued upriver. With their new home finally in view after five weeks of travel, they broke out in song, an Auca ballad being improvised for the occasion. The short, repetitive strains were always climaxed by a lusty yodel. Phrases that had been called from the plane during many of the flights inspired the Aucas and were now included in the verses. Two of the verses ran:

> I am Kimo, I am Kimo:
> My own "sons," my own "sons,"
> Come, O come, he says!
> *Yihoooooooo!*

I am Dyuwi, I am Dyuwi:
Baiwa's people, Baiwa's people,
Listen, O listen to God!
Happily, happily live, He says!
*Yihoooooooo!*

A triumphant Kimo and Dawa led them into Tiwaeno. Baiwa was wearing a parachute, with his head poked through the big hole at the top, one arm through another hole, and the rest of the parachute draped over his body. One man had devised a garment from the cloth that lined the electronic basket.

The Aucas chanted loudly the traditional songs that celebrated the end of a long journey. The men sang loudly in one thatched house while the women chanted joyfully in another. Dawa served drinks to the thirsty travelers, while Rachel welcomed them with generous offerings of bananas. Tiwaeno Aucas had gathered to greet the newcomers—but some of the downriver group had purposely gone to other clearings before their longtime enemy, Baiwa, arrived.

Laughing and talking, eating and singing, the historic reunion was a gala affair. Much of the conversation revolved around the marvelous basket and calls from the plane.

Had Baiwa actually heard Kimo's message to him from the plane, *not to kill the outsiders* stationed at the oil camps?

Yes, Baiwa said he had heard and heeded. He had *not* killed outsiders after that; he had only stolen their manioc.

# 14 ❧ POLIO!

Baiwa's group listened curiously as the Tiwaeno relatives told of God's Carving. Even Babae was amenable to some of the novel ideas introduced to the tribe through Dayuma and her foreign friend, Nimu. At least he displayed no hostility, no desire to separate *Nimu's* skin from her soul. She was glad she had befriended Babae's son, Cangowanto!

Dawa began to teach her relatives zealously, and she nursed the sick constantly. The newcomers were amazed at the readiness with which relatives swallowed foreigners' remedies, and at how they geared their lives to rules spoken by Father God.

For two weeks Dawa worked, scarcely eating or sleeping. Then on August 30 an emergency call came. A husky, handsome young man, Amoncawa, living with other downriver people on the Curaray, was very ill. Could Dawa go to his aid?

She left immediately. Upon arriving at Amoncawa's side, she found him alarmingly feverish and breathing with difficulty. Some of the symptoms resembled the flu that plagues Aucas upon initial exposure to foreigners' diseases. Dawa gave medication and left antibiotics for him before returning to Tiwaeno.

The next day word came that Amoncawa had died in the night. After Dawa left, his condition had worsened. He died drooling at the mouth, and with partial paralysis.

Iniwa, living near Amoncawa, added to the sorrow by attributing the death to witchcraft. He blamed Piyamo, a witchdoctor in the downriver group. Iniwa had been baptized on Palm Beach with Oncaye and Kathy and Steve Saint. But he had steadily regressed into the old ways of the ancestors, which included threats to kill those supposedly responsible for illness.

Sorrow followed sorrow. Rachel received the sad news from her family in the States that her mother, who had been ill for a month, died on September 2. Although Rachel knew that her mother was rejoicing with her Lord whom she had loved and served faithfully, she had lost her best prayer warrior at a needy time.

Within a few days Amoncawa's mother came to Tiwaeno with symptoms of her son's fatal illness. She lay suffering in her hammock in the shelter under Rachel's house. In spite of intensive nursing by Dawa and Rachel, she also died.

Alarmed, Rachel conferred by radio with Lois Pederson, the Wycliffe nurse at Limoncocha. Upon hearing the symptoms, Lois suggested the possibility of polio.

Polio! . . . Rachel gasped. Not polio to complicate an already complex situation! Poor Dawa! Would her brother, Baiwa, and his group, who were just settling in to a brand new foreign world, be exposed to this killing disease?

On September 7 Dayuma, who was working in her fields on the Curaray, radioed to report another death. A mother from Oncaye's group on Fish River had taken ill and was on her way to Dayuma for medicine, when she died on the trail, foaming at the mouth.

The entrance of the disease was traced to a group of Quichuas traveling down the Curaray and over to Fish River. They had stopped first at Amoncawa's place and shared manioc drink with the Aucas there, then continued to Fish River.

Soon others from the Fish River location became ill. A downriver family living there came to Tiwaeno for medical help, a man and baby already partially paralyzed. Gikita's daughter-in-law living on the Curaray also came to Tiwaeno with polio symptoms.

Worse than the disease was the news concerning Iniwa. Carrying out his verbal threat, he with the help of several other young rebels had speared the son of the witch-doctor, Piyamo. Stunned by the first spearing among them in twelve years, the

Tiwaeno Christians looked to God for His solution to a threatening situation. Dayuma guarded Iniwa day and night, fearing he would also spear Piyamo, and implored the downriver group not to avenge the death.

One week after the killing, Iniwa was near Palm Beach with some of his young companions when he suddenly fell to the ground, unconscious. He revived, stood up, and declared that he was all right. Again he fell, this time screaming and writhing for a short while—and died. He was buried near the place where he had been baptized.

God's judgment upon Iniwa stayed the plague of spearing.

In Tiwaeno the deadly illness began to spread rapidly. Tidonca's family was stricken; within a week four of them would die, last of all Tidonca himself. His fifteen-year-old son was the first to become violently ill and paralyzed. Knowing that he would die, he said to Tidonca, "Father, I'm dying, but don't weep for me the way our people weep. I have chosen the Jesus trail, and I am going to heaven." But as his son lay dying, Tidonca was sharpening his spears. He talked openly of killing his daughter if he lost a worthy son.

The lad died with a peaceful expression on his face. Tidonca, though very ill, prepared the corpse for burial by doubling the boy's legs against his chest and tying them to the body with a vine. He arranged on him his best armbands with ornaments of beautiful hawk feathers. Rachel recorded that "it looked like the Victor's crown for this lad who had gone to be with his Saviour."

Then the mother put the corpse on her back to carry it out of the house for burial. "My son! Oh, my son!" Tidonca cried in grief. As he followed his wife to the door, Rachel took the spear he had been making and started through the back door. "Nimu! Don't take my spear!" Tidonca called to her.

"You promised me you wouldn't use it," she answered, "and I'm going to see that you don't!"

The spear was hidden safely in Rachel's house, under her bed.

Within a few days Tidonca's stepson died, then one of his wives. His old mother, breathing heavily, also died.

When Tidonca himself had become very ill, a surviving wife began to dig a hole beside his hammock. She was planning to bury her husband before he died! When Rachel dissuaded her from digging further, she became angry, took her two young sons, and left.

Oncaye and Rachel fed and cared for Tidonca. Dyuwi stayed by his side and invited him to ask Jesus to wash his heart clean before he died. The words concerning the "great gulf fixed" between heaven and hell impressed him, and with his dying words he murmured a hope of seeing his son in heaven.

There were more days of sadness as one by one downriver people from Oncaye's and Baiwa's groups continued to fall ill. On September 28 Kimo's nephew died. The nephew's wife, who was Dawa's spitfire half-sister from Baiwa's group, became frustrated and rampageous in her grief. She bashed in all of her husband's belongings in the house, then burned the house to the ground.

Upon witnessing the tragic end of some of her people for whom she had risked her life, Dawa became despondent. She held up four fingers and declared, "If *this* many die, I'm through!"

Rachel reminded her that God's requirement is for faithfulness unto death, with no conditions. Dawa listened thoughtfully to the words from God's Carving and determined again to follow the Lord, regardless of the consequences.

Babae's wife died during the epidemic and he fumed. He announced that he would kill a man and capture a wife, and proceeded to make a very long spear. Rachel watched for an opportunity and lifted the spear. She had to break it to get it out of Babae's house.

"I did it with a prayer in my heart that the Lord would protect me, for I didn't know how Babae would react," Rachel recalls. "As God would have it, he did not react at the moment.

But long after the epidemic was over he said to me, 'Now you owe me a pair of pants for that spear you took!'—a low price under the circumstances.''

At the height of the epidemic when Rachel was doctoring the Indians day and night, she herself began to show symptoms of the disease.

"I remember when it hit me," she recounts. "The muscles in my arms and knees drew up all at once. I could feel them shrinking. All of a sudden I was unutterably weak."

But Rachel continued to minister to the other victims, praying for strength for herself.

On September 24 nurse Lois Pederson and Dr. Wallace Swanson of the HCJB Shell Mera hospital were flown into Tiwaeno to check on Rachel and other victims. No doctor or nurse —outsiders—had come in sooner because of the danger of spearing.

Dr. Swanson concluded that probably two kinds of polio were involved, with a predominance of bulbar, affecting adults. He found Rachel to be suffering from a mild case of the disease, which affected her muscles.

Lois was a friend to many of the Aucas, who had been treated at the clinic at Limoncocha. She stayed on in Tiwaeno for several weeks to care for the many patients, and improvised therapy for those who needed it. She devised bamboo poles for walkers and arranged successively heavier bunches of bananas to be lifted as an aid in strengthening muscles weakened by the disease.

One of the patients most seriously stricken was Oncaye. Rachel wrote in a letter of the girl's grave condition: "Oncaye almost died yesterday. We all prayed much. When she regained consciousness she said she had been in a beautiful place 'where Nimu's brother is.' After she had been at the point of death several times, the Auca elders anointed her with oil and prayed. At once she began to rally."

Oncaye recovered completely, with no crippling traces of the ordeal.

Some of the patients were taken to the Shell Mera hospital and put in iron lungs. Two of them died there, and a third, Enae from Oncaye's group, hovered between life and death for days. But she recovered and was able to recount that one day during her illness, she had heard Rachel speaking Auca on the radio set up in the room to help the nurses who did not speak the language of their patients. "Oh, if they are speaking Auca, I must still be in this world!" she had thought.

On another day she had "dreamed" she was skipping down a broad trail when suddenly she saw people swimming in boiling water and screaming. She ran back in horror on the trail and heard the two Aucas who had died in the hospital calling to her, "Enae! Take the narrow trail!"—but when she turned, the way was barred.

She asked what the "dream" meant. Dawa explained that there were two trails, one of which led to heaven. That trail had been barred to her because she, unlike the other two, had not yet let Jesus wash her heart clean.

In addition to the two who died in the hospital, fourteen died in Tiwaeno within five weeks. Three of the deaths were in Baiwa's newly arrived group, and thirteen in Oncaye's downriver group. A number of survivors were crippled by the disease, including the witch-doctor, Piyamo, and one of his sons. More severely paralyzed were Piyamo's nephew, Nanca, and Naenae, the son of Tidonca.

Christian friends in Ecuador and the States responded to the emergency by generously donating medical personnel and equipment including crutches and wheelchairs. Through Medical Assistance Programs, Inc., Dr. Juan Correa was sent to the Shell Mera hospital and spent ten days with the Auca patients. The organization also sent a thousand doses of Trivalent Polio Virus Vaccine, which helped to check the spread of the disease.

For weeks after the epidemic had begun to wane, Dyuwi worked all day with the disabled Aucas. He raised and lowered legs and kneaded flabby muscles to restore normal mobility, a monotonous ministry of mercy that he said God had told him to perform. Since he had no time to provide food for his family, he was helped by Gikita, who took hunting as his responsibility. The love of Christ had constrained these former killers to serve their fellow tribesmen from an enemy group.

The several nurses who came from the States gave many months to the Auca cause. Rosi Jung, a German Wycliffe member and a graduate midwife, assisted in the polio isolation ward in the Shell Mera hospital. Later, she went to Limoncocha to supervise therapy there, and eventually joined Rachel and Catherine in the tribal team.

Flights over the Ridge, which had been suspended for fear of dropping the deadly germs to the unreached savage relatives, were resumed in November, 1969. During one of these, when a successful basket drop had been made, Toña identified the voice of his sister, Omade, on the ground. From that day Toña was ready to leave immediately to bring her and her family out to safety.

Amid encouragement from the Ridge, however, came a devastating blow from Baiwa's group. Disheartened by the tragic polio epidemic and angered by a shortage of food, twenty-eight of the group led by Baiwa himself had run away from Tiwaeno for home. They were discovered by helicopter, and Kimo tried to warn them of oil exploration at their former home area.

Unconvinced, Baiwa and his runaways stubbornly refused to return. "Tiwaeno," Baiwa said, "is a *place of death!*" They continued downstream, into a jungle now crisscrossed by oil company trails and hundreds of "foreign" workmen.

# 15 ❧ SILENCE ON THE RIDGE

Toña the Tiwaeno teacher had had no pupils during September and October. His busy schedule performing deeds of mercy left time only for reading God's Carving to stricken Aucas. He urged them to ask for God's forgiveness before they died.

Fortunately, oil exploration in the area had a temporary lull. With the resumption of flights over the Ridge, Toña had spoken from the plane to almost all the locations, informing the large groups of people he saw in the clearings of the sickness in Tiwaeno. Oil company helipads would soon dot the surrounding jungle, and he asked them again not to kill anyone coming there.

As he awaited the day when he could learn more about his brother, Wepe, and his sister, Omade, Toña prepared for his visit to his relatives. He diligently improved his own reading and writing skill, and in mid-November he reopened the literacy school to continue teaching. Putting first things first, Toña began the class with prayer to Father God, then read from God's Carving. He carefully copied the verses on the blackboard and taught them to his pupils. Then he turned to the patient labor of guiding rugged hands, accustomed only to handling blowguns and spears, to carve Auca characters on paper. A born teacher, Toña set his own teaching patterns and shouldered his responsibility with devotion and initiative.

On November 20 a basket transmitter was dropped at the clearing where the exciting clues about Wepe and Omade had first been discovered. It now brought confirmation that Omade was alive, and that Toña's brother, Wepe, lived on another clearing. Toña was overjoyed.

On follow-up flights in December the Aucas on the clearing spread out the big white parachute and shook it violently as they shouted for gifts. But the transmitter was not destroyed and for many weeks vital information about Toña's people were recorded on tapes. Each flight increased Toña's desire to see his people face-to-face. On one of them he actually spoke with Omade, after which he said to Rachel, "My sister, Omade, is out there. I must go to tell her about God."

There was a temporary delay in Ridge contacts because of the transfer of polio patients from the Shell Mera hospital and Tiwa-eno to Limoncocha. There Dr. Swanson's brother, Ellsworth Swanson, of Santa Ana, California, established a rehabilitation center for them. He introduced a program of therapy that Aucas could adapt. Toña visited the patients at Limoncocha occasionally, to offer invaluable help and to encourage them to turn to God for salvation and comfort.

Toña's trip to the Ridge also had to be delayed. When he had spoken to Omade about visiting her, the Auca fear of outsiders made her hesitate. That *Thing* from which he talked was no Auca possession! And Toña knew that the many strong men on the Ridge were killers.

Finally, in early April, 1970, Omade gave permission for the visit, but with the understanding that he arrive by trail. Toña, however, arranged to go as close as he dared by helicopter.

Toña was at Limoncocha on April 27. The big day set for the Ridge operation was closed in with rain. While he waited for the weather to clear, Toña composed a note to Rachel, the first correspondence in the Auca language. Anticipating his meeting with his older brother, he wrote as follows:

"Because of your sincere prayers to God, He is going to work wonderfully for me. While I was yet in Tiwaeno, God spoke to me: 'You go, and having gone and carried them all my message, then after they have heard, whoever says "Yes!" will believe.'

"They should come first to Limoncocha. Then after they come and have been clearly taught about God, we will take them to Tiwaeno. After they have been taken there and think favorably concerning God, then we shall say, 'God, You have done well!'"

Toña signed the note, folded it, and added a request for his family: "Out of love for God, please secure an ax for me and give it to Wato's child. Wato"—and here the note ended abruptly because the oil company helicopter had broken through the clearing fog to whisk away the author.

Hasty plans were made for the plane to fly to Omade's clearing, drop gifts, and circle as Dyuwi called from the plane. Meanwhile, the helicopter would drop Toña at a nearby cleared field a short distance from Omade's house. Rachel interpreted the pilot's instructions for Toña. He then practiced on the airstrip at Limoncocha, expertly lowering his radio by rope and jumping from the helicopter with his small pack. Pilot Bob Conway observed that his only passenger was an alert, agile Auca who would perform well on target.

The helicopter took off first. The plane carrying Rachel and Dyuwi caught up with it over the jungle and led the way to the manioc patch where Toña would land. Then it circled over Omade's well-populated clearing on the Ridge. As the attention of Omade and her family group was diverted by the plane's loud roar and the blast of Dyuwi's calling over the loudspeaker, the helicopter bearing their close relative slipped unnoticed down among the trees that surrounded their manioc patch not far away. But to the great consternation of the pilot, the reported "clearing" was small and blocked by one tall tree in the middle. Toña apparently saw no problem, for he motioned the pilot forward. *What? into that tree?* No, this was the end of the road, and the pilot could do nothing to maneuver the helicopter any lower than twenty feet from the ground.

At a nod from the pilot Toña lowered his radio, then jumped without hesitation. Conway continued to watch, not without some anxiety, as Toña brushed off the dirt, shouldered his radio, and began to pick his way toward the edge of the clearing. Apparently, nothing but a few manioc stalks had been broken by the impact. Now the lone youth was scrambling over the brush at the edge of the patch, and Conway saw him pause just before slipping out of sight into the forest. He was waving a last good-by. *Imagine a man's stepping voluntarily into such solitude—and peril!*

Back at Limoncocha, Bob Conway, long experienced in treacherous jungle flying and marginal landing pads, could express nothing but admiration for Toña's careful performance. Knowing that this was but the beginning of a high-risk mission, Bob wished him God's protection.

The next day Toña reported by radio his previous night's experience. Since he was not sure of the trail, he had prepared to spend the night alone in the manioc field, praying for God's guidance. About midnight he heard the commotion of men returning on the trail from a wild hog hunt. Upon hearing the name of his brother, Wepe, he picked up his gear, followed the group to a small house, and waited outside in the shadows. When he was certain of his brother's identity, he gave the Auca call to announce his presence—and Wepe invited him in!

The reception was warm. How good it was to see his own brother! And soon Omade, at a nearby house, would be coming to see him!

Each day Toña called in on schedule to Rachel with an enthusiastic report: "Today, I told them of the Creator God . . . Today, I told them that God had an only Son, and His name was Jesus! How surprised they were to hear that name!"

On successive days he taught them of David, God's man who did not spear his enemies. He told them of Tiwaeno, the community of peace where Auca relatives lived according to God's Carving. Each day he read the Gospel of Mark to them. He also told his people of the need to learn to live with foreigners in peace.

Occasionally, he asked for a flight to bring a few axes, machetes, and beads for his relatives.

One day he reported that he would be going to another clearing to give serum to a man named Dyuwi, who was dying of a poisonous snakebite. He called back later to say that he had administered two vials, which had saved the man's life. As he kept vigil through the night, he talked to him about God's Carving.

When Dawa heard the news she wondered if the man could be her brother, Dyuwi, whom she had not seen since he was captured as a small child.

Late in May Toña reported that a big party would be given at Wepe's clearing. The older Aucas in Tiwaeno knew that at the party there would be a review of the hatred of foreigners who came out "like stars at night." The party would perhaps end in a wedding, or *something worse.*

On June 5 Toña called in to say that there was trouble and that he might have to flee in the night. Rachel and the Aucas in the therapy hut in Limoncocha and those who received the report in Tiwaeno were deeply concerned. But during the next morning's message he stated that he had talked with God all night and was told to stay and teach his people; he therefore would not leave.

While anxiety for Toña mounted, there was a happy interlude. Rachel and all the polio patients were flown home to Tiwaeno where Dyuwi would head up the therapy program. From the new therapy unit set up under Rachel's house the patients listened for radio reports from Toña.

Several days later Toña's mother, Miñi, who was apprehensive about the coming party, talked with him by radio. She told him that her little granddaughter missed him and hoped her father would return home soon. His bashful wife, Wato, and their small daughter were called to the radio. Addressing the little girl affectionately, Toña said, "Praying very, very much to our Heavenly Father, He accomplishing it, I will come home to you again."

On June 25 Toña did not call in, nor on the next day. The silence was ominous.

On the third day Dawa was flown from Tiwaeno and over the clearing with Catherine. They found only charred ruins of houses, with no sign of life. The high hopes of Toña, as well as of the Tiwaeno Christians, seemed destined for ruin. Heartsick, Dawa asked to fly over her sister, Cawo's, clearing. It too was burned to the ground.

"Now I will never see Cawo again," she said.

When they flew over the clearing to the east, the bright aluminum pots received as gifts in the electronic basket were turned upside down on top of deadly spears.

"Two hundred Ridge Aucas had disappeared overnight!" was Catherine's bleak report.

# 16 ❧ RETURN OF
## THE RUNAWAYS

Following the mysterious disappearance of Toña and of Wepe's large group, several search flights were made. Trails were watched in vain; there was no visible human activity in the silent forest below.

Omade's clearing was still occupied and a basket transmitter was lowered. Information about Toña was sketchy and dubious. He had fled, some said. No—he had returned. Others said he was dead.

By the fall of 1970 reports reached Tiwaeno of threatening signs placed by Aucas on the oil company trails moving eastward in the lower Curaray area. There was only one answer: Baiwa and his runaways were the only Aucas now living in that part of the jungle.

Dayuma, who was concerned for her sister, Omatoki, Baiwa's wife, declared that she would go and plead with the rebels to return.

Early in December Rachel and Dayuma were flown in an oil company helicopter to Baiwa's river home, where Dayuma's strong admonitions were heeded reluctantly. The runaways would return to Tiwaeno if they, too, could come partway by helicopter!

To expedite the move, a helicopter airlift from Baiwa's location to the oil camp on the lower Curaray was arranged with oil officials. On December 12 Rachel and Dawa joined the operation. Two small helicopters shuttled frightened Auca women and children, as well as an apprehensive Baiwa and his companions, to the abandoned oil camp.

From their river camp some of the Aucas now saw an awesome monster racing down the Curaray toward them. Horrified, they screamed to Rachel, "Nimu! What kind of animal is it?"

The "animal" was a huge motorized canoe. This roaring beast would take them upriver "without poling"! A second motorized canoe arrived a little later.

On the eve of the adventuresome trip by motor, Baiwa's group tried to sleep on the banks of the Curaray. It was their first night out of Auca territory, and only the children slept. The Auca men, some of whom had recently speared outsiders, were extremely nervous and listened for the snap of every twig in the forest.

The next day the Indians and their gear, and Rachel with her gear, along with sacks of rice and stacks of bananas for the trip, were loaded into the two canoes. Then the noisy engines were warmed up and the runaways were soon bouncing upriver. They were terrified but excited by the new and thrilling mode of transportation.

At nightfall, cold and soaked by jungle rains, they stopped to make camp. Early the next morning they continued the trip and reached a large encampment where oil workers and Ecuadorian military men were stationed. Word had preceded the arrival of the unique expedition, and Ecuadorian military men were on hand to greet the Aucas with peace offerings. The children were presented with huge dolls—just in time for Christmas!—and the women were given big, shiny cooking pots. Baiwa, grinning from ear to ear, very happily received a bright new machete and other gifts.

The roaring canoes, heavily laden with "foreigners' " things, started to resume the journey up the Curaray. Quichua Indians who were living in a river village saw the motley load of passengers and recognized them as Aucas. Aucas—the hated killers who had speared their people along this very stretch of river through the years! Soon an eerie Indian death wail rang from the riverbanks, rising higher and higher. Quichuas were remembering and announcing the presence of the Aucas with a growing crescendo of grief.

"Let's get out of here *quick!*" Dawa said tensely to Rachel.

Sensing the danger, the Ecuadorians in charge of the encampment quickly dispatched a two-motorboat escort to protect the Auca expedition past the last Quichua house where the piercing death wail was heard. Once out of the danger zone, the escort waved farewell and returned downriver.

The expedition slept that night on another beach. On December 15 the group reached a spot near the mouth of the Tiwaeno River. Arrangements had been made by radio for Upriver Dabu to meet them with a canoe. When he did not appear, the Aucas became impatient. A few of them decided to walk up the beach to a shallow spot, where they started to cross the river on foot. Soon the whole party followed. But the river began to rise suddenly, swollen by upriver rains. The swiftness and depth of the current made crossing treacherous.

"Let's get Nimu over there *quick!*" the Auca men said protectively. They guided Rachel through the rushing river, which came up to her neck. Women, their huge pots held over their heads, also hurried across, while strong Auca men carried the children, who clutched their foreign dolls, to safety. Finally the men, some of them wearing colorful gift helmets, carried the last load of gifts and provisions across the river that by now had become a thundering, muddy horror.

Single file, the parade of Aucas started toward the Tiwaeno River. They trudged through damp and unmarked forest, a series of lakes complicating the way.

Suddenly, the parade halted while the leader studied the ground.

*What was he doing?* Rachel wondered. She learned that he was trying to determine which way the water drained on the ground, for he was unsure of the direction to travel. With the growing darkness, the leader admitted they were lost.

Rachel brought out her compass. Then, after conferring with

Dawa and receiving her approval, she offered it to the group. Would they like to follow its leading? They agreed. With this guide Rachel was able to bring them out on the Tiwaeno about five o'clock, as darkness fell.

The Aucas were quite impressed with the compass. "Without it, we would probably still be out in the forest somewhere!" Dawa said.

The next day Dabu finally found the wanderers, and they began the last trek to Tiwaeno. Dawa and Rachel went in Dabu's canoe to a helipad up the Tiwaeno, where it had been arranged by radio that a helicopter would fly them home to the Tiwaeno village.

En route to Tiwaeno the group stopped at the fields of On-caye and her husband, who were living some distance from the village. They were welcomed and fed. Since they knew that Dawa would pass on word of their recent attacks on outsiders, the group wanted to delay the scolding they expected to receive from their families in Tiwaeno. They therefore tarried there about two weeks before continuing the journey.

Their arrival at Tiwaeno was subdued. It lacked the journey's-end joy that had sent chants of jubilation throbbing through the thatched huts when they first came the year before.

"There was nothing of that, and there was quite a different tone to things!" was Rachel's summation of the second Baiwa mission—accomplished.

# 17 ❧ "IF YOU ARE TOÑA, CARVE FOR US!"

Conversations with Wepe early in 1971 via electronic basket revealed little concerning Toña's whereabouts. Tiwaeno relatives, suspecting that he had been killed, spoke of their fears to Wepe, who challenged them, "If you don't believe Toña is alive, send my own daughter, Oncaye, in to find out!"

Clues leading to certain proof of Toña's death were pieced together by Catherine, who wrote:

"It has been one year since Toña leaped from a hovering helicopter to bring Christ to his brother Wepe's family. This whole missionary tale since his disappearance in late June is written only in hidden jungle trails, or perhaps in an overgrown gravesite.

"Taped evidence that he still lived at Christmas time was confirmed. We saw him with our own eyes waving from the clearing we were circling, and calling to us on the radio transmitter. We saw him with our own eyes—or did we? We heard his voice on tape—was it not truly his voice? We had no doubt that it was really Toña. Calling to him on the loudspeaker, we made arrangements with him to bring him out. His brother, Wepe, asked only that his very own daughter, Oncaye, bring machetes and axes in her hands to him. Then he and Toña would return to Tiwaeno together. It was all very clear. Had they not cleaned off a crude area for the helicopter to land?

"They landed—Oncaye and her baby, her brother, Tewae, and the helicopter pilot of the oil company who cooperated in the effort. Oncaye and Tewae were well received, they reported to us by radio, and made arrangements for the pickup, first for Toña and Wepe, and later for themselves.

111

"We covered these dangerous operations, circling overhead in a JAARS plane, calling instructions to the people on the ground on a loudspeaker and advising the chopper pilot by radio when to land. He was delighted to see that Tewae had directed the people in the construction of a real helipad in a much more reasonable location. The first two passengers were quickly whisked away.

"We arrived in the plane on the oil company airstrip before the chopper, and I set up my camera for a picture of Toña. But I never took the picture. Could that be Toña climbing out of the helicopter? No! Certainly not the first one! Then it must be the second. No! That one looked *less* like Toña! Maybe it was the first one after all! Could he possibly have changed so much? What he must have been going through!

"I recovered enough to speak to them. After all, I was the only person there who spoke their language! The older man immediately introduced himself as Toña's brother. The whole thing looked perfectly convincing—but the whole thing was a big hoax, a wildly improbable impersonation. I went along with it until we reached Tiwaeno. . . . "

Wato was among the eager crowd of Aucas waiting anxiously on the Tiwaeno strip for a first glimpse of the passengers from the Ridge. As the plane rolled to a stop, the door opened and two Aucas emerged. One called out, pointing to his companion, "Here's your husband—take him home!"

Wato took one look at the younger man, who began to pale and tremble with fear, and exclaimed, "That's not *my* husband!"

The crowd went wild, with everyone shouting at once as Wepe insisted that this *was* Toña!

"Where did you get those big earholes?" someone asked angrily. "Our Toña had none!"

"I liked the way the ancestors had them, and I had mine done the same way," was the weak answer.

"Not *those* big holes in *that* short time!" was the quick reply.

"If you are *our* Toña, where are your alligator bites?" was another challenge.

"I cut my leg with a machete, and the bandage is right over the alligator toothmarks. Don't touch it—it *hurts!*"

With this unconvincing answer the taunting crowd burst into uproarious laughter.

As the relatives plied the Ridge men with more questions, Miñi had run home for a picture of her son, Toña. Now holding it close to the new "Toña," she said proudly, "This is what *my* Toña looked like—not *this!*" And she pointed scornfully to the younger "brother," now paler and shakier.

Someone appeared with a pencil and paper and thrust it at "Toña."

"*Our* Toña knew how to carve on paper very well. If you are Toña, *carve* for us!" screamed the challenger.

Someone else handed him a copy of the Gospel of Mark and demanded, "If you are our Toña, read to us as you used to in our God's-speaking-house!"

With this "Toña" slumped to the ground, beads of perspiration glistening on his face.

In the confusion that followed, Wepe said something about Toña's having been *changed;* tribal sorcerers brought people back to life in a different form.

Dayuma, who had joined in the angry challenge to the two lying Ridge men, turned to her relative, Wepe, and spoke sternly:

"Wepe, you listen to me! *Our* Toña loved Father God very, very much. No witch-doctor in the *world* could change him into this miserable creature!" And she pointed down to "Toña," still sitting weakly on the ground.

She was certain that a lying spirit had possessed Wepe, and she rebuked it quietly, in the name of Jesus. The reaction was instantaneous: Wepe raced down the airstrip and away from the crowd!

Indignant at the deceit staged clumsily by Wepe and his own

son, Kiwa, the Tiwaeno people ridiculed the two unmercifully. The imposter "Toña" bore no resemblance to *their* beloved Toña! Wepe's weak defense, that one of Kiwa's names was "Toña," was rejected with scorn.

Wato, now certain that her Toña had been killed on the Ridge, was comforted in caring for her new son, Gaba, who looked "just like his father." She knew that through Toña's death, for whatever cause, wild relatives like Wepe had heard the words of God's Carving. Someday, believing, they would follow Him.

Baiwa's group bristled with anger. There were now many of them, and they focused their attention on the lone Wepe. Since he had killed some of their relatives and captured others, they were wary of his presence among them.

"Wepe has come for the last time . . . he will never see home again!" they shouted as they hastened to the forest to make chonta spears.

Dayuma, after learning of the design on Wepe's life, hurried to the area where Baiwa and his men were chopping the hardwood palm. She addressed them fearlessly:

"Listen to me, you fellows! *You* killed my brother and my uncle, and I'm not crying about it! I protected you from the oil company, I fed you with my own food, I clothed you when you wanted clothes. *Now you let Wepe alone, I say!* Dropping your spears, *you let Wepe alone!*"

The lecture shamed the men, and they feared the wrath of the Tiwaeno group. Returning sullenly to the village, they sulked in their hammocks.

Wepe, uneasy about Baiwa and confronted by the community that had penetrated his deception, lost some of his bravado. One day as he was standing by the edge of the porch to listen to tapes that told of the judgment of God, and upon seeing for the first time a map indicating the advance of oil trails in a network surrounding his Ridge home, he swooned and fell into the mud. As he was being "brought to" with nettles, he murmured, "Fearing for my children I got fainthearted."

Within a few days Wepe asked to be taken back to the Ridge, with his nephew, Monga. Wepe had promised his daughter to Monga, whose wife, Boika, had died a year earlier.

He refused to say any more about Toña, and, leaving his son, Kiwa, in Tiwaeno, left with Monga.

Monga and Wepe had scarcely settled in after hiking eastward from the nearest helipad into the Ridge when a frantic call for help came from the survey party in the area. Aucas had speared a cook at an oil camp on that same line, but far to the west of the helipad. Pilot Bob Conway poured out the story that night at the base camp:

"When I got into the helipad it was too near dark to rescue all the survivors or to fly out the body. Eleven men scrambled all over the helicopter, begging to be flown out. I forced some of them to wait, and did something I was sure I'd never do: allowed two passengers to stand on the sleds and cling to the outside, so I could shuttle four at a time to the next helipad and still make it back here to base camp by pitch dark."

Next morning Kinta flew with Catherine and JAARS pilot Virgil Gottfried to circle and call to Aucas who might still be lying in wait at the scene of their attack. Conway and another pilot flew in a crew of workers who recovered the mutilated body, along with some two dozen spears that had met their cruel mark.

*Could Wepe have turned so soon to spear again?* No mention was made to Monga by radio other than a diligent inquiry into the whereabouts of Wepe's and Omade's relatives. All were accounted for, and circumstancial evidence led Kinta and the Tiwaeno Aucas to conclude that the spears were thrown by "others." And the only other Aucas known to roam the forest were the few in the splinter group who had suffered at the hands of Oncaye's relatives and remained behind when that group left for Tiwaeno in 1968.

"Oh!" Wepe said when he heard of this later. "It must be the same crowd of 'others' who attacked us the year before Toña came in ... " And a flood of spearing stories unloosed, paralleled by later stories, from *other* sources, of Wepe's retaliatory spearing—all within the past three years.

During the crisis in Tiwaeno several of the old standbys who had helped absorb other shocks were missing. The growing demand in the States for firsthand information concerning the Auca tribe found Rachel, along with Kimo and Dawa, Gikita and Sam, sharing their story in a series of spring rallies.

While in the States, they were invited to appear on NBC's *Today* show, where former killers Kimo and Gikita informed millions of viewers of the miracle that had changed them. Gikita, very live and in color, and typified by huge empty holes in earlobes once filled by balsa plugs, spoke of having speared several men, including Rachel's brother. But his heart had changed ever since he heard God's Carving. Following Father God, he would never kill again.

The impact of Gikita's simple, forceful testimony moved many viewers, as well as the personnel of the *Today* show who interviewed the unique missionary panel.

Dayuma meanwhile bravely held the fort, encouraged by Catherine Peeke and Rosi Jung. Her own growing family now demanded much time and energy. There were four small children to care for. Nancy, old enough to be mother's helper, often forgot her waterpot at the river where she chased big beautiful butterflies! Her sister, Eunie, blind from birth, always cheered the family with her sunny smile. Alert and willing, Eunie learned to help her mother with manual chores. Eva, their beautiful younger sister, spent her time amusing baby brother

Solomon, Dayuma's pride and joy. Komi spent his time providing jungle game for the family and tending his growing herd of Brahman cattle started by Heifer Project.

Since Dayuma knew that she was appointed by God to help Rachel complete her priority project, the translation of the Auca New Testament, she looked for Rachel's return. God's whole Carving was needed for the rapidly growing Auca church as savage kinsmen brought into Tiwaeno believed and identified themselves with "God's-believing-family." It was with great enthusiasm, therefore, that she welcomed Rachel, who had taken a brief furlough after the missionary party was brought back from the States in April.

# 18 ❋ "HEARING, HE WILL BELIEVE GOD'S CARVING"

Following his return to his Ridge home, Wepe with Monga's help had started to clear an airstrip similar to that in Tiwaeno. Since they had constant radio contact with Tiwaeno, Monga one day asked that his radio be replaced because the signals were weak.

"Oncaye agreed to go in for a few hours, make the radio replacement, give a short course in behavior toward outsiders, and make suggestions toward airstrip construction," Catherine recorded. Dawa, eager to see her relatives, volunteered to accompany Oncaye. Upon hearing this, Miñi said that Dawa should not go; she was Toña's relative and she too would be killed! But Dawa nevertheless decided to make the trip.

Oncaye and Dawa, with a lift in the oil company helicopter, went to the Ridge. They returned without incident and with a glowing report of cordial reception.

Catherine continued:

"Omade and her sons were at Wepe's, recounting their experience of fright when oil crews came quite close and made so much noise. Their account agreed with what we had seen from the air: they had chopped down their banana trees, burned their new house, and fled, never expecting to return.

"They confessed quite openly that they had been the ringleaders in spearing Toña last year, saying that they would never have done it if they had not been misled into believing he was an outsider.

"Would Dawa and Oncaye forgive them? . . .

"Yes, because of God's mercy, and the fact that Toña is in heaven, they would."

Omade, half-sister to Wepe and Toña, had said that her sons

killed Toña without her knowledge. And her husband, Nampawae, had acted as the decoy to get Toña out into the jungle —she grieved very much about that.

As Dawa had prepared to leave the Ridge, her brother, Dyuwi, whose snakebite Toña had treated, called her to his hammock. He wanted her to teach him more about the Lord. He said, "I am a very sick man and will not live another month. I want to know more about the Lord before I die." Dawa told him, "You don't need to die! I will speak to the Lord about you daily, and He will make you better!" She taught him more, and sang an Auca hymn for him.

Dawa had been disappointed by Cawo's doubt that they were sisters. "Just look at my face!" she said. "It is just like yours!"

Within a few weeks after Dawa's visit, word came by radio that Dyuwi was dying. On July 30 he and his family were brought out by helicopter to the nearest airstrip, then on to Tiwaeno by plane. The traumatic experience for these Ridge people who had never left their wooded world was recounted by Catherine:

"The frightened subjects swooped in by helicopter, draped with white parachute material to keep out the terrifying sights and sounds. I had a time coaxing them to take that long step down to the ground, with the rotor still whirring and a multitude of strange people gathered around to watch. Dyuwi's children were clinging to their mother, screaming."

Pilot Roy Gleason, who had flown many dangerous hours over the Ridge, helped Catherine and Dawa comfort the family and fly them to Tiwaeno.

With the arrival of her brother, Dyuwi, Dawa was surrounded by all of her living brothers and sisters except for Cawo, wife of the powerful sorcerer Awaemae. Her prayer for Kimo's salvation, which extended to include *all* her family, was being answered!

In time Dawa was given an eyewitness account of Toña's death. He had been literally chopped with an ax in the back and fell to the ground. "I'm not afraid. I'll just die and go to heaven,"

Toña said. "We'll help you go, then," his killers jeered. "As for us, we don't want to go." And they surrounded him with poised spears. Still conscious, Toña told them again of God's love. "I forgive you," he said, "and now I am dying for your benefit."

As the first Ridge family settled into Tiwaeno, another emergency call came from Monga. Uncle Iketai was dying, he said. Could the "big bird" come to his rescue *immediately?*

Again it was Pilot Gleason who participated in the shuttle operation. Dr. Catherine Peeke—doctor in *linguistics*—quickly assembled her medical kit as she and Kimo prepared for the trip. While waiting for the plane, Catherine jotted in her diary:

"To think that today I am to land on the very spot I saw burned and deserted last year—the long Ridge clearing that I even then dared to ask the Lord to give as an airstrip to reach those fugitive killers! And I will have the joy of treading on the nearly completed airstrip being constructed just yards away from the site I had claimed by faith! How I have longed to drop down among them, instead of circling by the hour over their heads! And today, suddenly, I have that joy!"

After they reached the sick man and ministered to his physical and spiritual ills, old Iketai brightened enough to look up and say:

"Let me get a good look at you, Sister. Give me a drink of water so that I may drink from your hand and revive!"

He had his wife fill a little gourd cup with water, which Catherine held to his lips.

"Now I'm revived! . . . If you hadn't come, I would have died!" he said.

Catherine learned that Iketai was a powerful witch-doctor on the Ridge. Grateful for her help, he promised to abandon his threats toward outsiders.

The Ridge people proudly showed Catherine where they were clearing big trees for the airstrip.

"This is the plot that *my* family cleared—all of this!" one said. "And here is where *we* cleared!" said another.

Early in November Dayuma and Komi went to the Ridge to check progress on the airstrip. It was almost ready, thought Dayuma, who had supervised the construction of the Tiwaeno airstrip.

Tewae had spent a week in September; and Coba, with his wife, Gakamo, spent two weeks in October, assisting in the backbreaking work of clearing huge trunks and stumps. Now Komi remained for a week to help with the final stages and to escort Wepe out.

On November 9 the Gaba River airstrip, located near the Ridge river for which it is named, was inaugurated by JAARS pilot Virgil Gottfried. On that notable occasion Roy Gleason and Virgil flew Wepe, his two wives, and some of their many children to Tiwaeno to live. Wepe received a special welcome from his real daughter, Oncaye, as well as from Dayuma and Rachel, both of whom call him "father."

Tiwaeno Christians now plant manioc for Ridge kinsmen invited to join Dayuma's growing group. Fifty harassed Ridge Aucas have come to the Auca Protectorate where they hear words of eternal life from God's Carving. Two hundred more Indians still roam the Ridge, untamed and untaught except for what they learned from Toña.

Gikita, long concerned for his witch-doctor brother, Awaemae, seen only before spearings separated them as small children, has planted a big patch of manioc. It is for Awaemae and Cawo—enough for their extended family. It is growing well. Gikita recently reported to Rachel that the manioc would be ready just at kapok season, when Dayuma and Komi go to teach the people on the Ridge. "Returning, they will bring Awaemae with them. Coming, Awaemae will eat manioc with us in Tiwaeno. Hearing, he will believe God's Carving."

 LIST OF NAMES

(B., Baiwa's group; D., Downriver; U., Upriver; R., Ridge)

Akawo (U., ah-*cah*-woh) mother of Dayuma

Amoncawa (D., a-mohn-*cah*-wah) son of Piyamo; first to die in polio epidemic

Awa (D., *ah*-wah) younger brother of Oncaye; son of Titada

Awaemae (R., a-*wam*-a) half-brother of Upriver Gikita

Babae (B., *bah*-ba) half-brother of Dawa; brother of Baiwa

Baiwa (B., *bah*-e-wah) half-brother of Dawa

Boganai (D., boh-gan-*nay*) mother of Cangowanto, the son of Babae; stolen as wife by Niwa; speared after Niwa was killed

Boika (D., *bwee*-cah) grandmother of Oncaye; speared before Oncaye fled

Boika (U., *bwee*-cah) wife of Monga; half-sister of Oncaye; died in 1970

Caiga (R., *cah*-e-gah) half-brother of Upriver Gikita's father; father of Wepe's wives; brother-in-law of Toña's father, Coba

Cangowanto (D., cyang-oh-*wahn*-toh) son of Babae and Boganai

Cawo (R., *cah*-woh) sister of Dawa; wife of Awaemae

Coba (D., *coh*-bah) father of Toña, Wepe, and Omade; speared when Toña was a little boy

Coba (U., *coh*-bah) husband of Gakamo; grandson of Downriver Coba

Dabu (D., *dah*-boo) "the Rebel" son of Niwa

Dabu (U., *dah*-boo) brother of Kimo and Maengamo

Dawa (U., *dah*-wah) wife of Kimo; first Auca Christian, after Dayuma

Dayuma (U., dah-*yoo*-mah) Auca Christian leader; Rachel Saint's translation helper; married to Komi

Dyuwi (R., *dyoo*-wee) brother of Dawa

Dyuwi (U., *dyoo*-wee) Auca evangelist; married to Oba, sister of Dayuma

Enae (D., *en*-na) half-sister of Dayuma; widow of Downriver Gikita

Eunie (U.) blind daughter of Dayuma; died by drowning in 1972

Eva (U.) youngest of Dayuma's three daughters

Gaba (U., *gah*-bah) son of Toña, born after Toña's death

Gaewa (R., *ga*-wah) son of Caiga; brother of Wepe's wives

Gakamo (U., gah-*cah*-moh) half-sister of Oncaye; married to Upriver Coba

Gikita (D., ghee-*kee*-tah) brother of Piyamo; died of polio

Gikita (U., ghee-*kee*-tah) brother of Akawo

Iketai (R., ee-ke-*tay*) married to Caiga's daughter

Iniwa (U., en-*nee*-wah) son of Wiba; later adopted by Akawo; died after spearing during polio epidemic

Kimo (U., *kee*-moh) Auca Christian leader; married to Dawa

Kinta (U., *keen*-tah) foster son of Upriver Gikita; married to Ana, half-sister of Dayuma

Kiwa (R., *kee*-wah) son of Wepe; married to Omade's daughter; impersonator of Toña

Kogi (B., *coh*-ghee) Dawa's brother who fled when she was captured and brought upriver

Komi (U., *coh*-mee) son of Upriver Gikita and Maengamo; husband of Dayuma

Maengamo (U., man-*gah*-moh) wife of Upriver Gikita; sister of Kimo

Minkayi (U., meen-*cah*-yee) half-brother of Dayuma

Mintaka (U., meen-*tah*-cah) aunt of Dayuma; half-sister of Akawo

Miñi (U., *meen*-yee) mother of Toña; later married to Upriver Dabu

Moipa (U., *mwee*-pah) former enemy of Dayuma's household; speared downriver during Dayuma's absence from tribe

Monga (U., *mohn*-gah) nephew of Wepe and Omade; husband of Upriver Boika

Naenae (D., *nan*-na) married son of Tidonca; paraplegic from polio

Nampawae (R., nahm-*pah*-wa) husband of Omade

Nanca (D., *nahn*-cah) son of Downriver Gikita; married to Biba, daughter of Upriver Gikita; paraplegic from polio

Nancy (U.) oldest daughter of Dayuma and Komi

Nangae (U., *nahng*-a) husband of Oncaye; son of Upriver Dabu

Nimonga (U., nee-*mohn*-ga) half-brother of Upriver Coba; married to Dayuma's half-sister, Upriver Wiña

Nimu (D., *nee*-moh) aunt of Oncaye; shot by outsiders

Nimu (*nee*-moh) Auca name of Rachel Saint

Niwa (D., *nyee*-wah) half-brother of Dawa; husband of Titada; killed by outsiders after Oncaye fled

Oba (U., *oh*-bah) sister of Dayuma; wife of Upriver Dyuwi

Omade (R., oh-*mah*-de) half-sister of Toña; married to Nampawae

Omatoki (B., oh-mah-*toh*-kee) half-sister of Dayuma; married to Baiwa

Ompoda (U., ohm-*poh*-da) wife of Minkayi; half-sister of Oncaye

Oncaye (D., ohn-*cah*-ye) daughter of Wepe and Titada; wife of Nangae; key figure in downriver and Ridge contacts

Ongimae (D., ohng-*ee*-ma) oldest daughter of Titada and Niwa

Piyamo (D., pee-*ya*-moh) son of Dawa's half-sister; his three wives are dead; left on crutches by polio

Sam (U.) grown son of Dayuma

Solomon (U.) baby son of Dayuma

Tewae (D., *te*-wa) brother of Oncaye; married to daughter of Upriver Dabu

Tidonca (D., te-*don*-cah) half-brother of Oncaye; died of polio

Titada (D., tee-*ta*-dah) mother of Oncaye; widow of Niwa

Toña (U., *tohn*-ya) Auca missionary martyr; son of Downriver
 Coba and Miñi; married to Wato

Tyaento (D., *tyan*-toh) oldest brother of Oncaye

Wato (U., *wah*-toh) Toña's widow; daughter of Upriver Boika's
 brother, Gaba

Wepe (R., *wep*-pe) half-brother of Toña; son of Downriver
 Coba; Oncaye's father

Wiba (U., *wee*-bah) half-sister of Oncaye; married to Upriver
 Dabu

Wiña (D., *ween*-ya) wife of Tyaento

73 74 75 10 9 8 7 6 5 4 3 2 1